Creating Our Own Lives

Creating Our Own Lives

COLLEGE STUDENTS WITH INTELLECTUAL DISABILITY

Michael Gill and Beth Myers, Editors

University of Minnesota Press
Minneapolis
London

This work was supported by the Lawrence B. Taishoff Center for Inclusive Higher Education and the Center on Disability and Inclusion at Syracuse University.

Published by the University of Minnesota Press
111 Third Avenue South, Suite 290
Minneapolis, MN 55401–2520
http://www.upress.umn.edu

Available as a Manifold edition at manifold.umn.edu

ISBN 978-1-5179-0971-0 (hc)
ISBN 978-1-5179-0972-7 (pb)

A Cataloging-in-Publication record for this book is available from the Library of Congress.

Printed on acid-free paper

Part III
Inclusion as Action: Diversifying Student Experiences 115

19. Hi, I'm Jake Miller 117
Jake Miller and Katie Ducett

20. "BGWYN" and "Confidence with Curves" 129
Taylor Cathey

21. Inclusive College Education 132
Micah Gray, with Karlee Lambert and Lydia Newnum

22. My UC Perspective 136
Joshua R. Hourigan

23. Phoenix Nation as in Spirit 139
Cleo Hamilton

24. My Excel Story 144
George Barham

25. #CreatingMyOwnLife 146
Payton Storms

26. Inclusive College Education 150
Makayla Adkins

27. My Story about Aggies Elevated at Utah State University 153
Brenna Mantz Nielsen

28. Questions and Answers 157
Lawrence Sapp

29. College Memories but Ready for What's Next 162
Amanda Pilkenton

30. Full Year of College 166
Luke Wilcox

31. My Favorite Memories in College 170
Elizabeth Droessler

Part IV
Supporting Growth: Peer Mentoring and Support 173

32. Communicating Successfully in College 175
Maia Chamberlain

33. True Rafferty Interviewed 177
True Rafferty, with Nathan Heald

34. College Program Experience 183
Gracie Carroll

35. Teaching, Assisting, Reflecting: Our Experience Working Together 185
Phillandra Smith and Meghan Brozaitis

36. My Georgia Tech Excel Story 195
Maggie Guillaume

37. Emma's Journey 202
Emma Miller

38. Come Read about My Awesome Journeys through Life 205
Brianna Silva

39. My Social Experience throughout Georgia Tech 207
Rachel Gomez

40. The Importance of Goals 210
Tyler Shore

41. Support and Encouragement for the Ones Who Seek It 215
Elliott Smith

Coda: Why This Collection? 219
Beth Myers and Michael Gill

Acknowledgments 225

Contributors 227

This book is dedicated in memory of inclusive scholar Megan Cartier and for all the students who will carry on her work.

to caroline
from Antonio

Contents

Introduction: Recognizing Student Voice in Inclusive Higher Education xi
Michael Gill and Beth Myers

Part I
Laying the Foundation: Why Everyone Belongs in College 1

1. I Want to Go to College 3
Antonio E. Contreras

2. I Got In 10
Taylor Ruppe

3. Adventures in Postsecondary Education 11
Stirling Peebles

4. A Language to Open 18
Adam Wolfond

5. "The Wanderer" and "This Is What I Sing" 25
Steven Brief

6. My History of the Excel Program 28
Alex Smith

7. Taking the Llama for a Walk and Other Things That Helped Us 32
Olivia Baist and Kylie Walter

Part II
Opening Up Possibilities: Overcoming Doubt and Uncertainty 51

8. Being Independent Has Risks: How to Recover When Something Terrible Happens 53
Kailin Kelderman, Eilish Kelderman, and Mary Bryant

9. Spartan Kid: Journeys 68
Brandon Baldwin

10. Best Experiences at IDEAL 79
De'Onte Brown, Deriq Graves, Nadia Osbey, Breyan Pettaway, and Sayid Webb

11. Two Poems 83
Carly O'Connell

12. Goal(s) in Common 84
Hannah Lenae Humes

13. I Did What They Said I Couldn't 87
Allen Thomas

14. Climbing Higher and "From Mission Impossible to Mission Possible" 89
Courtney Jorgensen

15. Inclusive College on Zoom? My Inclusive Higher Education 2020 Experience 91
Stephen Wanser, Kate Lisotta, and Kim Dean

16. Inclusive College for All and How My Perception of My History Prof Changed 97
Keiron Dyck

17. Qua's GT Excel Life and "Never Give Up" 101
Marquavious Barnes

18. Photo Essays and Selections from Student Leadership Conference 2019 104
Breana Whittlesey, Kaelan Knowles, Elise McDaniel, Kenneth Kelty, Katie Bartlett, and Rachel Mast

Part III
Inclusion as Action: Diversifying Student Experiences 115

19. Hi, I'm Jake Miller 117
Jake Miller and Katie Ducett

20. "BGWYN" and "Confidence with Curves" 129
Taylor Cathey

21. Inclusive College Education 132
Micah Gray, with Karlee Lambert and Lydia Newnum

22. My UC Perspective 136
Joshua R. Hourigan

23. Phoenix Nation as in Spirit 139
Cleo Hamilton

24. My Excel Story 144
George Barham

25. #CreatingMyOwnLife 146
Payton Storms

26. Inclusive College Education 150
Makayla Adkins

27. My Story about Aggies Elevated at Utah State University 153
Brenna Mantz Nielsen

28. Questions and Answers 157
Lawrence Sapp

29. College Memories but Ready for What's Next 162
Amanda Pilkenton

30. Full Year of College 166
Luke Wilcox

31. My Favorite Memories in College 170
Elizabeth Droessler

Part IV
Supporting Growth: Peer Mentoring and Support 173

32. Communicating Successfully in College 175
Maia Chamberlain

33. True Rafferty Interviewed 177
True Rafferty, with Nathan Heald

34. College Program Experience 183
Gracie Carroll

35. Teaching, Assisting, Reflecting: Our Experience Working Together 185
Phillandra Smith and Meghan Brozaitis

36. My Georgia Tech Excel Story 195
Maggie Guillaume

37. Emma's Journey 202
Emma Miller

38. Come Read about My Awesome Journeys through Life 205
Brianna Silva

39. My Social Experience throughout Georgia Tech 207
Rachel Gomez

40. The Importance of Goals 210
Tyler Shore

41. Support and Encouragement for the Ones Who Seek It 215
Elliott Smith

Coda: Why This Collection? 219
Beth Myers and Michael Gill

Acknowledgments 225

Contributors 227

Introduction

Recognizing Student Voice in Inclusive Higher Education

Michael Gill and Beth Myers

What is inclusion? On some level this is a fairly straightforward question that demands a similarly straightforward answer. Inclusion means being considered part of a group. In our work, we often talk about inclusion connected to education: true inclusive education means that all students are welcomed into the school and classroom community and are fully supported in their educational process.[1] Yet, we know that what is labeled as inclusion can change drastically from one school or program to another. Some models in which disabled students are paired with students without disabilities in a separate camp or after-school program might be called "inclusive." Low expectations of students with disabilities means that at other times inclusion might be more symbolic—for example, including students with disabilities as members of a club or team without changing any of the structures to allow for meaningful participation. Sometimes these students are called "buddies" or "peers." We would argue that being a softball manager, in name only, does very little to challenge how ableism and discourses of pity or "specialness" further create separation between the student with disabilities and their peers.

Oftentimes when thinking about inclusion, there is a focus on being in the same space regardless of disability. A performance of a play can be considered inclusive if captioning, ASL, audio description, barrier-free seating, and other relevant types of access are embedded as part of the planning and performance. But is the theater inclusive if access is dependent on an individual requesting it first? Inclusion is often considered only when the student with a disability attempts to enter a space, to go through the door to the school building or classroom with their peers. It is at this moment that educators and administrators (and, ideally, family and the student as well) address the best way to meet the needs of the student. Yet, we often know there can be a large disconnect between what works or what is assumed to be possible and what is the best approach for the student and their community. More often than not, what is called "inclusive" might only be in name and not practice. As we tell our students, most models of inclusion still depend on someone opening the door to the space. Gatekeepers (such as administrators) can have the final say, despite laws that might codify the right to education. Is it inclusion if someone is only allowed to enter because someone else says so?

Inclusive higher education can be understood, then, as a battleground on what counts as, or, frankly, who belongs in, higher education. To be explicit, often individuals advocating for inclusive higher education programs are faced with the most reductive, ableist assumptions that students with intellectual and developmental disabilities do not belong on college campuses. Behind this line of thinking is a belief that focusing on making higher education more welcoming, more accessible for all, will upset the rigor and prestige that many college campuses base their reputations upon. As of mid-2023, there are 318 inclusive higher education programs in the United States, which represent a variety of campuses and styles of colleges, including private universities, liberal arts colleges, and community colleges. Many of these programs are creating opportunities for students that previously could not access higher education. Students attending these programs are receiving education that prepares them for careers as, for example, teaching assistants, prep cooks, office administrators, library staff, and groundskeepers. While attending these programs, students are often given opportunities to expand their skills of independence, learning to manage schedules, commutes, and deadlines.

The range of programs can cater to a wide variety of interests and desires from potential students. Some programs offer vocational training, while others allow students to audit classes on a variety of topics from African American contemporary literature to journalism. Some programs are built on a cohort model where all students take workshops together, while others allow students to tailor their own schedules. There are programs that allow students to live on campus, while others do not. Behind each of these differences reflects a decision about what type of program will be available for students with disabilities. While these programs all might be labeled "inclusive," we know that opportunities to interact with matriculated students outside these programs might be limited, or even seemingly impossible. Others might even try to allow or facilitate interactions with matriculated students, but the students in the inclusive programs might choose to socialize, go to the dining hall, and generally hang out only with students in the program. Colleges can be fascinating locations of social interaction presenting opportunities to meet many others that do not share your own life experiences, yet, at the same time, there are many opportunities to form collectives around common experiences, including sexual orientation, racial status, and religious practice. The distinction is often whether students are given the opportunity—and supported—in finding others to join in community. We know that some inclusive higher education programs are not inclusive but rather still largely segregate students in separate programs on campus. We also know that disabled students might chose to socialize with each other because of affinity, but also because campuses can be ableist spaces that do not accept their ways of being as valuable.

In a 2022 article, Meg Grigal, Clare Papay, and David R. Johnson provide an overview of inclusive higher education.[2] They discuss how there are roughly only six thousand students with intellectual disability enrolled in higher education programs in the United States. (There are almost nineteen million college students in the United States.) Of the total number of students taking classes, 62 percent were enrolled in inclusive classes with matriculated students and only 28 percent were earning college credit.[3] In their article, they raise important considerations about how accessible inclusive higher education is for BIPOC students with intellectual disability and how individuals can pay for college. Sometimes, depending on the program, students might be able to utilize Medicaid waivers or vocational rehabilitation funds to help pay for programs, but some opportunities remain out of reach for students without the funds to afford tuition and fees. Barriers remain that prevent students from accessing inclusive higher education, including rigid funding, lack of scholarships, and recruiting patterns that favor white, middle-class students and those with significant home resources and support. In this collection, we have sought a diverse group of students to include the experiences and perspectives of disabled students of color to challenge the assumptions of some about which types of students are accessing these programs. As a collective of educators and administrators, we have much work to do to continue to challenge these structures that prevent many disabled students of color from accessing programs.

In this collection, we have brought together students from a variety of inclusive higher education programs to share their own experiences. In doing so, we shift the focus away from higher education experts and those without intellectual and developmental disabilities. This collection is the first of its kind. Directly asking students with labels of intellectual and developmental disabilities about their college experiences—including their dreams, desires, heartbreaks, and experiences of exclusion and violence—affords the opportunity to nuance our discussions of inclusion. Are inclusive higher education programs meeting the needs of students? In what ways do these narratives illustrate that students are entering college ready to take full advantage of the resources available to fulfill their dreams? What lessons do these narratives offer the next generation of students wanting to go to college?

Inclusion as Method

There is a popular meme that our students often bring to class. On the left, in the first frame, three children are positioned outside center field trying to look in and watch a baseball game.[4] A fence is in front of these children. They are each standing on a wooden box, with the word *equality* written below it. Each child is given an equal number of boxes, but not all can see; in fact, one of the children is quite tall and one is not. The shortest child can only see the fence, not the game. The second frame illustrates the same three boxes and three children, but the resources have been redistributed to achieve what is called "equity." Indeed, now all children can see the game. The tallest child does not have a box to stand on, the shortest child has two, and the middle child stands on one box. This frame is measured as equity by our students because all three children are at the same height because of the boxes. The meme illustrates how educators should focus on the outcome of resource distribution to achieve something that can be assumed to be equal.

We challenge our students to think beyond this framing of the solution as a more equitable distribution of boxes. Certainly, students that need supports should receive them, but merely passing out support in the name of equity still might not challenge any structural systems that prevent meaningful participation. The fence still exists. These three children are still positioned outside the baseball stadium. The logic that some (those that can pay the price of admission) belong inside and some belong outside is not challenged in the proposed solution. Rather, we ask our students to consider what justice or revolution might be if we applied those principles to this example. There are many examples of how individuals have taken the original meme and modified it for their purposes.[5] When asking the students to consider what justice might be for this meme, many talk about removing the barrier of the fence. If the fence were to disappear, the three children could still enjoy the baseball game, but on their terms. Standing, crawling, sitting, on boxes or not, the three will have an unobstructed view, provided they access baseball using many senses, including sight. What was created to get individuals to think about how equal resources can be shared might actually bolster models that reinforce structural inequality. We ask our students to imagine how their classroom and community spaces will continue to be segregating if fundamental structures and assumptions are not challenged.

Sharon Brown, Imani Evans, and Regina Watts discuss how historically Black colleges and universities have not yet expanded offerings for inclusive higher education, except for Alabama Agricultural and Mechanical University.[6] The article mentions other programs—including TigerLIFE at the University of Memphis and the Leveraging Education for Advancement Program at Albany Technical College in southwest Georgia—that enroll a large percentage of students from historically underrepresented populations. The U.S. Office of Special Education Programs documents how Black students are overrepresented in special education, including as having labels of intellectual disabilities.[7] Yet, as Zeus Leonardo and Alicia A. Broderick argue, "By conceptualizing the problem as one of overrepresentation, there is a risk of tacit reification and legitimation of the naturalness and neutrality of the bureaucratic system of special education as a whole, and by extension, of the deficit driven and psychological understandings of 'ability' and 'disability' within which it is grounded."[8] Our work in advocating for more opportunities for disabled students of color requires a deep examination of how practices of inclusion and delivery of special education services continue to fail multiply marginalized students. Instead of only advocating for more accurate assessments, which, as Leonardo and Broderick argue, can make these assessments seem valid and neutral and not a product of the oppressive structures, we ought to make sure that in advocating for inclusive higher education, we center the experiences and perspectives of disabled students of color to help challenge white supremacist structures that seek to frame these students as not belonging or enhancing college campuses. In this collection, we feature many disabled students of color and their experiences to challenge the narrative that inclusive higher education is only for white middle-class students with Down syndrome or autism.

In thinking about special education and the power of labeling, one of us, Michael, asks students in an introduction to disability studies course to think about their early messages about what constitutes disability. During this process, Michael talks about two memories that approached disability in two distinct ways. As a child, Michael attended a program for "gifted children" that was held in a school where students with disabilities were bused to. He attended this program once a week. The students in the "gifted program" had very little interaction with the students with disabilities. One of the clearest efforts to create a spatial distinction between the groups of students occurred in the lunchroom. On the floor of the lunchroom was a painted line that literally demarcated forced separation: disabled students in special education on one side and the "gifted" (and presumably nondisabled) students on the other side. (There was an implicit assumption that there were no disabled students in one program and no "gifted" students in the other.) Regardless of the reason for the separation, violence was accomplished by this choice. Michael learned that his peers with disabilities supposedly belonged on one side of the room and everyone else on the other. Any effort toward inclusion or to address complex experiences as students with disabilities and multiple identities was erased with the line on the ground. We can agree that this was not a model of inclusion, although all ate lunch in the same room.

This history of segregation has taken a harsh toll on people with intellectual disability and many other disabled communities. Today, opportunities for employment are abysmal, as roughly

34 percent of working-age adults with intellectual disability are employed nationally. Only half of those who are employed are working in competitive employment, while the rest are in sheltered or segregated work arrangements.[9] Students that complete a Transition and Postsecondary Program for Students with Intellectual Disabilities (TPSID) are employed at a much higher rate (67 percent, three years postexit).[10] While more longitudinal data can support the claim that postsecondary programs provide opportunities for employment, we do know that many students that finish programs find careers that help enable them to manifest their dreams and desires.

Educational statistics are equally poor, as only 19 percent of students with intellectual disability spend 80 percent or more of their school day in inclusive settings with their nondisabled peers. Students with intellectual disability are in the largest category of disability to be included for less than 40 percent of the school day, sometimes in completely self-contained classrooms with no interaction with school peers or the general education curriculum.[11] More often than not, students with intellectual disability continue to encounter educational and service delivery that segregates them based on their disability label. Disabled students of color, students from low socioeconomic backgrounds, and students with labels of "severe" disability face additional barriers that prevent them from accessing inclusive educational and employment settings. We also know that students in segregated settings are often not given opportunities to apply for the inclusive higher educational programs. The path to college is often blocked by placements in segregated spaces and low expectations of academic achievement.

Fortunately, the tide is changing, as increasing numbers of young adults with intellectual disability are actively constructing their own futures. Empowered by generations of self-advocates and robust disability rights movements, individuals with intellectual disability are gaining entry into locations that were previously marked as off-limits. The students featured in this collection are part of this first generation of students that are demanding access to college. A number of colleges and universities are creating programs for students with intellectual disability, initiatives that afford the opportunity to audit college courses with their peers while preparing them for entrance into the competitive workforce. Think College, a national coordinating center for transition and postsecondary programs for students with intellectual disability, maintains a database of 318 programs across the United States.[12] One example, Inclusive U, run by the Taishoff Center for Inclusive Higher Education at Syracuse University, is a multiyear program where over one hundred students are currently enrolled. Six years ago, students began living in the dorms on campus, bringing their experience closer to that of their traditionally enrolled peers. As additional programs expand and this generation of students enters the workforce, a new era of inclusion will emerge. Many of the students featured here discuss their desires for careers, living independently away from family, getting married, having children, being active alumni and ambassadors of their colleges, and inspiring future generations of disabled students to enter into college. We are excited to learn from the authors in this collection as they seek out avenues for advocacy to make higher education less oppressive and more welcoming for a diversity of learners.

College is a place of learning, taking risks, and imagining your future self. Anyone with a college-aged student, or working in higher education, can appreciate that some students, regardless of disability, seem to have it all figured out, while others languish, remaining uncertain of what the future holds even after graduation. Some of us major in one field, only to take jobs in a completely different arena. Michael's students are surprised to learn he transferred colleges four times during his undergrad. In the narratives that follow, many students express ambitions to become professional photographers, actors, fashion designers, and educators, to live independently, get married, and have children. Many of these ambitions are like those of matriculated students. Yet, we know that individuals with labels of intellectual disabilities face barriers in employment, while guardianship or consent laws might make it very difficult for them to achieve goals of independence, getting married, or having a family. The students we work with at Syracuse University often understand the restrictive systems they must navigate. We discuss eugenics, ableism, and paternalism in our workshops and classes. What is our responsibility as educators to prepare students for the reality that their dreams might shift or not be met? How do we remain optimistic about inclusive opportunities and still prepare students for the extensive advocacy for self and others they must engage in to realize their dreams in an ableist world?

As mentioned earlier, employment outcomes are higher for students completing TPSID programs. During the time of working with the authors in this book, we have learned that some were able to achieve their employment goals as photographers or working with animals, for example, while others have had a series of jobs at gyms, restaurants, and childcare facilities. Other students have gotten engaged and are living independently. Others adopted dogs and cats. We believe that inclusive higher educational programs prepare students with intellectual disability to better navigate ableist systems that continue to frame their desires as unrealistic, yet we are also keenly aware that many will fail or make mistakes. As educators, we can prepare our students to be equipped to help actualize their dreams, while continuing to push back against ableist systems that construct those with intellectual disability as forever unable or incompetent. We presume competence for our students and understand that they can be, and are, in charge of their own lives.[13] Our students get to decide what constitutes a meaningful life for themselves, and that might be different from how others define that meaning. The ableist views of exclusivity in higher education continue to create barriers, but these individual and collective stories push against that traditional narrative.

We know that only a small fraction of all eligible students with labels of intellectual and developmental disabilities enrolls in inclusive higher education programs. Some of the programs are intentionally small; others might be cost prohibitive. Higher education is still seen not as a right but rather as a privilege for the select few. Annual tuition increases, reduced financial aid, and private and exclusive institutions only exacerbate this distinction. Many programs are concentrated geographically, and the only available option might be hundreds of miles away from a student's hometown. Others might be inclusive in name and not practice, meaning that students have little to no opportunity to interact with matriculated students. There remain serious sustainable challenges for these programs, including consistent university support and the ability to scale up programs to meet the growing demand. Quite simply, many more inclusive programs are needed.

In discussions about higher education, many people think that only those who are supposedly smart or have a decent SAT score belong. (We do find the decisions by some schools of forgoing SAT and GRE scores in discussions of admissions hopeful, but we are also cautious that other standardized mechanisms will still be utilized.) One of the often-unchallenged assumptions about higher education is that including students with intellectual and developmental disabilities will somehow taint the educational experience of the students without these disabilities. Behind these criticisms is often a belief that students with intellectual or developmental disabilities do not belong in higher education. We disagree completely.

Another memory Michael shares is one he also talks about in the preface to his book *Already Doing It*.[14] As a child, Michael's favorite babysitter was labeled with an intellectual disability. At the time, he did not know her disability labels, just that he wanted his parents to leave so she could come over and watch him and his siblings. In the home, disability was unnamed and, importantly, his parents did not consider disability to be a barrier to taking care of three young children. As disability studies scholars committed to challenging interlocking systems of oppression, we recognize that inclusive higher education programs can work to dismantle university enrollment policies that have reinforced exclusionary practices where nonwhite students are merely assumed to be targeted for their diversity. We contend that for far too long, students with labels of intellectual and developmental disabilities have been assumed not to belong or to enhance universities and colleges. Universities remain ableist, racist, and exclusionary spaces for many students. As la paperson explains, we can make the university a space of freedom and liberation for those previously excluded by diverting resources and programs.[15]

Published works on inclusive postsecondary education remain scarce, but new understandings are emerging. Much of the research that does exist is focused on program development or employment outcomes in order to bolster pleas for additional funding. What is largely missing from the research in inclusive higher education are the voices of the students themselves. That is why this book is necessary. *Creating Our Own Lives* presents student narratives of their experience in order to challenge assumptions that intellectual disability is best met with protection or segregation. This collection is written by students themselves to explore the following questions: How do young adults with intellectual disability experience higher education? How do opportunities in inclusive higher education provide access to skills and knowledge that enable individuals to take control over their futures? How does the interdependent nature of these programs, where students interact with peer mentors and direct support professionals, challenge assumptions of the necessity for grit and meritocracy? What do the experiences of students with intellectual disability tell us about the potential of inclusive postsecondary programs? The stories of the students themselves address these core questions. Readers may notice these themes emerging as the book progresses, and we circle back to a reflection on these questions in the final chapter.

In this volume, the authors are sharing their experiences and perspectives on higher education. Some of the pieces are written in conversation with friends or peers. Others are written by individuals. The authors have used Google Docs, voice recognition, word processing software, speech-to-text apps, Zoom, FaceTime, and many other technologies to capture their experiences and expertise. One constant refrain through the multiyear process of putting together this book was "anything goes."

As college students were navigating remote learning and the Covid-19 pandemic, many were finding themselves learning from home, or dorm rooms, while trying to remain connected to their friends and classmates. Some of the student narratives talk about a wish for the pandemic to be over so they can return to campus or meet their friends in person. Others entered college during the pandemic, having to figure out complex structures while trying to reduce their exposure. Although we will not know the full impact of pandemic learning for some time, many students faced extensive barriers during the rush to transition online in the spring of 2020. Some inclusive higher education programs were paused abruptly or closed altogether while matriculated peers were able to continue online. Some students did not have access to the learning management systems of the university because of their student status, and others had to exit internship or employment opportunities. Many lost hard-won levels of independence, moving home with family and isolating from friends. Supports had to be reimagined for those who were able to continue their university work online.[16] When colleges and universities were all trying to respond to the changing public health landscape, students with intellectual disability were not always centered.

Embedded in this collection is a flexibility grounded in a belief that everyone has a story to tell and share. Labels of intellectual disability do not make these stories irrelevant or inconclusive. Sometimes the mode of telling shifts or requires a different set of tools, but a key guiding principle remains: disabled students belong in higher education. This book (and the accompanying Manifold site) serves as an archive of the first generation of students enrolled in inclusive higher education programs. We invite you to explore the essays at your own pace, moving in and out of the selections as you explore the perspectives of the authors. There is no one way to approach this collection, but we are confident that no matter where you start, you will find valuable perspectives on the meanings of college, inclusion, dreams, support, and success.

Creating Our Own Lives is ensconced in a disability studies framework and utilizes methodological models of narrative inquiry. Narrative as a mode of telling recognizes that knowledge can be shared through stories and memories. Traditionally, people with intellectual disability are assumed to not be reliable storytellers or witnesses. These assumptions are not only incorrect but ableist. In forwarding narrative inquiry in this field, we seek to prioritize individual experiences of meaning-making to challenge these assumptions. We also explicitly challenge assumptions that a collection like this is "not scholarly" or only for a small percentage of readers. Certainly, these essays, and additional resources online, benefit current and future students enrolled in and preparing for college. Their parents, families, and larger support networks can approach these perspectives imagining what success can mean for students with labels of intellectual disability. Higher education administrators, special education teachers, and other practitioners can read these essays that invite us to critically examine our own assumptions while strategizing ways inclusive higher education can be expanded.

In the conclusion to her book *Autobiography on the Spectrum* Beth writes about how all students can be makers of experience and self-representation. She specifically says that disabled students "create meaning and their own understandings of the world."[17] She continues, "We need to create spaces where we can work with autistic teens to endure hatred, resist oppression, and reframe the dialogue on autism. We need to create spaces for youth to form alliances, push one another, and hold one another up. We need to create spaces for them to represent themselves as agents for change."[18] All people have the ability and the right to be makers in their own lives and tellers of their own stories. We can make space for those stories to be told in a variety of ways that honor the storytellers and value the stories. The testimonies that are shared in this book are immersive works that allow us to understand inclusive postsecondary experiences from an insider perspective, and that view is inherently valuable, despite a historically ableist devaluing. It matters that this work is being published and made available by a university press. In doing so, the University of Minnesota Press is making an explicit political statement that ableist assumptions of who belongs in college ought to be challenged; indeed, this work becomes part of a growing body of literature that centers experiences of marginalized and undersupported students challenging higher educational diversity talk about inclusion. The students here are sharing that being included in name only does not work; it is not inclusion. Meaningful and lasting inclusion is hard and sometimes fraught with contradictions, but ultimately it can enable less oppressive and more equitable higher educational experiences for all.

As inclusive higher education continues to emerge, this work is critical to the postsecondary field. This collection provides a view of the college experience from the standpoint of students with intellectual disability. It foregrounds the first-person perspectives that are often overlooked. This collection has the potential to change how we view higher education and the students who comprise it. Taken individually, each chapter offers a unique view of the college experience. Taken together, this work has the potential to change the face of higher education toward a more inclusive approach.

One of the unique opportunities this collection afforded was a freedom to work with as many student authors as we could possibly connect with. We posted calls for authors on social media and through outreach across the country. We contacted inclusive postsecondary programs and asked Think College to send out flyers on our behalf, recruited authors at the Student Leadership Conference, and even held our own author workshops. On a few occasions, we contacted specific students who we knew might have a particular story to share. We met weekly throughout this process to discuss student submissions and highlight any gaps we felt were missing in the narratives and perspectives. There were weeks (and seasons) where we felt that things were stalled. It was at these moments even more student writing emerged in our inboxes from programs throughout the United States. Poems, interviews, photo essays, and the like began multiplying. And without overstating things, we were blown away by these student authors sharing their inclusive higher educational experiences. Many of these experiences are what could be considered positive; these students find college a rewarding experience filled with opportunities for social and professional connections. Yet, there are other experiences that highlight how students enrolled in inclusive education can at times face ableism from professors that refuse to make reasonable accommodations or form rigid policies that only offer some opportunities for matriculated (degree-seeking) students.

We have collected these works throughout the book in a purposeful arrangement, primarily by theme: "Laying the Foundation: Why Everyone Belongs in College," "Opening Up Possibilities: Overcoming Doubt and Uncertainty," "Inclusion as Action: Diversifying Student Experiences," and "Supporting Growth: Peer Mentoring and Support." The first section opens with a straightforward but controversial claim: No one should be excluded from higher education because of disability. We recognize that not everyone accessing this text might agree with this claim. It is our hope that readers can shelve their doubts while accessing these pieces. Sometimes our imaginations need permission to dream. We encourage all to take the time to read and experience these pieces. With the necessary supports, we believe higher education can be attainable for individuals with labels of intellectual disability. The pieces in this section advocate for the expansion of inclusive higher education programs. They discuss the need to let students live on campus, have meaningful opportunities to learn, and be challenged, while also being given chances to fulfill their dreams.

The second section, "Opening Up Possibilities," continues this advocacy while also discussing how students, like their peers without intellectual disabilities, are taking full advantage of opportunities presented in college, including internships, scholarship programs, and student government. (These students are also partying, hanging out with friends, and going to football games on campus, too!)

The third section, "Inclusion as Action," includes student perspectives from a variety of social and political locations. The students discuss how they succeed once given institutional supports, including peer mentors and a diverse curriculum.

In the last section, "Supporting Growth," the students are offering advice to their peers with the goal of motivating other students to expect that college can be part of their plan. Of course, we should note that the divisions we made are not absolute, for example, as students might be addressing the benefits of peer mentors, while also discussing how everyone belongs in college. There are threads that weave throughout and patterns that return again and again. As editors, we have tried to refrain from overinterpretation, leaving the pieces to speak for themselves and in concert with one another. We do offer minimal notes on a few essays for background. In addition, on the Manifold site, the students offer pictures and other supplemental materials. (In the printed book, the Manifold icon appears in the margin of essay pages when more is available at the Manifold website.) We made choices of what to include and how to include it. We also worked on multiple rounds of revisions over email, text message, and Zoom sessions with the authors. All throughout, we worked with one goal in mind: foregrounding the experiences and perspectives of the students. We believe this is the most meaningful way to discuss the importance of inclusive higher education. We believe that these experiences, and their stories, challenge the assumptions about including (and excluding) students with intellectual disability in college. These stories tell the real truths about inclusive postsecondary programs. We end the collection with a brief reflection about the importance of this work and our hopes for future collections and partnerships.

Taking inspiration from the leadership of Alice Wong and the work she undertook in making *Disability Visibility: First-Person Stories from the Twenty-First Century* accessible to many, we are pleased to offer a discussion guide that accompanies this text.[19] Similar to the work that Naomi Ortiz completed for *Disability Visibility,* readers can find a discussion guide on the Manifold site.[20] Also on the Manifold site, readers can find photographs, videos, podcasts, and other multimedia self-representations that cannot be reproduced in the written text. Approach this text in ways that work for you. You can pick it up, read a bit, and then put it back on the shelf. Or start in the middle. Or the back. You can write your own experience in response to one of the chapters. Share your stories with others. And with us. We are eager for diverse groups of students, professors, administrators, and troublemakers to continue this work in additional collections, websites, documentary films, art exhibits, op-eds, and the like.

The students that are sharing their work talk about problems with roommates, a desire to find romantic partners, worries about employment after graduation, and struggles to gain independence from families and siblings. None of these concerns and experiences are unique to students with intellectual disability. And at the risk of being too didactic, we consider that to be one of the benefits of this type of collection. College students with labels of intellectual and developmental disabilities enrolled in inclusive higher education programs share many similar concerns with their nondisabled peers. Inclusive programs can be prepared to meet the needs of these students by enabling them to have the resources and support offered to all students.

We would be remiss, however, if we didn't also call on administrators and program coordinators in these inclusive programs to critically examine our own practices. How are we still upholding models that jeopardize the academic and social success of the students in our programs? Segregated classes, an inability to access campus resources (including scholarships, housing, and student organizations), and mentoring models that might mean having someone decades older than the student accompanying them around campus can all reinforce separate tracks and ableist exclusions. We expect that truths enclosed in these pieces will provide the impetus to continue working toward more inclusive, less oppressive futures. Quite frankly, even those of us that consider our programs a success might still be reinforcing segregation; we can all do better.

Part of the work we do at the Taishoff Center for Inclusive Higher Education involves supporting the national Student Leadership Conference, now in its fifth year as an expert gathering of college students with intellectual disability. At this conference, it really feels like inclusive higher education has arrived. These students are not merely settling for access to classroom—or campus—spaces. Rather, these students are demanding that colleges and universities address their legacies of exclusion and practices that assume students with intellectual and developmental disabilities do not belong in college classrooms. We have seen inclusive higher education opportunities in every state in the United States, as well as several countries across the world. We now have our very own academic journal for the field, the *Journal of Inclusive Postsecondary Education,* and a National Coordinating Center at Think College, and our professional and student conferences are thriving.

But this is only the beginning. We have a tremendous amount of work to do. There are 318 programs, up from just 25 in 2004, yet they still only represent 6 percent of colleges and universities in the United States. The largest programs—84 students, 100 students, or more—are in universities of 15,000, 30,000, or 50,000 students, representing such a small percentage of the overall student population. This work is valuable, energizing, cutting-edge, and worthwhile. This is work that matters in the world. Sometimes we forget because we are wrapped up in budgets, Title IX regulations, administrative procedures, and data collection, on top of teaching, learning, grant writing, publishing, and everything else on the to-do list. These students are leading the way, pioneers in the field of inclusive higher education. It is our responsibility to amplify their stories and push for change.

Notes

1. "What Is Inclusive Education?," Inclusive Education Canada, https://inclusiveeducation.ca/about/what-is-ie/.

2. Meg Grigal, Clare Papay, and David R. Johnson, "Inclusive Higher Education: Assessing Progress toward Better Futures for College Students with Intellectual Disabilities," *Impact* 35, no. 1 (Spring 2022): https://publications.ici.umn.edu/impact/35-1/inclusive-higher-education-assessing-progress.

3. Often, students enrolled in inclusive programs will audit, or take a class not for credit or a grade. When students finish these programs, they might receive a certificate. This works for some but not all. There need to be more opportunities for students to receive degrees.

4. Sometimes these are three children of color. Other times the children are represented by three distinct colors: red, blue, and yellow. The various memes try to address access to education (and resources) that has historically been largely unavailable to BIPOC students with and without disabilities.

5. Craig Froehle, "The Evolution of an Accidental Meme: How One Little Graphic Became Shared and Adapted by Millions," Medium, April 14, 2016, https://medium.com/@CRA1G/the-evolution-of-an-accidental-meme-ddc4e139e0e4.

6. Sharon Brown, Imani Evans, and Regina Watts, "Perspectives on Equity in Inclusive Higher Education," *Impact* 35, no. 1 (Spring 2022): https://publications.ici.umn.edu/impact/35-1/perspectives-on-equity.

7. "OSEP Fast Facts: Black or African American Children with Disabilities," IDEA: Individuals with Disabilities Education Act, August 26, 2020, https://sites.ed.gov/idea/osep-fast-facts-black-or-african-american-children-with-disabilities-20/.

8. Zeus Leonardo and Alicia A. Broderick. "Smartness as Property: A Critical Exploration of Intersections between Whiteness and Disabil-

ity Studies," *Teachers College Record* 113, no. 10 (October 2011): 2,208, https://doi.org/10.1177/016146811111301008.

9. Gary N. Siperstein, Robin C. Parker, and Max Drascher, "National Snapshot of Adults with Intellectual Disabilities in the Labor Force," *Journal of Vocational Rehabilitation* 39, no. 3 (2013): 157–65.

10. Grigal, Papay, and Johnson, "Inclusive Higher Education."

11. "Fast Facts: Students with Disabilities, Inclusion Of," National Center for Education Statistics, https://nces.ed.gov/fastfacts/display.asp?id=59.

12. "College Search," Think College, https://thinkcollege.net/college-search.

13. Douglas Biklen and Jamie Burke, "Presuming Competence," *Equity & Excellence in Education* 39, no. 2 (2006): 166–75.

14. Michael Gill, *Already Doing It: Intellectual Disability and Sexual Agency* (Minneapolis: University of Minnesota Press, 2015).

15. la paperson, *A Third University Is Possible* (Minneapolis: University of Minnesota Press, 2017).

16. Clare Papay and Beth A. Myers, "Inclusive Higher Education in the Time of COVID-19," *Journal of Inclusive Postsecondary Education* 2, no. 2 (2020): https://doi.org/10.13021/jipe.2020.2834.

17. Beth A. Myers, *Autobiography on the Spectrum: Disrupting the Autism Narrative* (New York: Teachers College Press, 2019), 91.

18. Myers, *Autobiography on the Spectrum*, 92.

19. Alice Wong, ed., *Disability Visibility: First-Person Stories from the Twenty-First Century* (New York: Vintage Books, 2020), https://disabilityvisibilityproject.com/book/dv.

20. Naomi Ortiz, "Discussion Guide for *Disability Visibility: First-Person Stories from the Twenty-First Century*," Disability Visibility Project, June 30, 2020, https://docs.google.com/document/d/1mWz84Ro0cq5YEPfg2-gXoR-B-T1fCWEIqz_0yZXs1jU/edit.

Part I

Laying the Foundation

WHY EVERYONE BELONGS IN COLLEGE

This first part of the collection contains essays from students about belonging and inclusion. Here, we introduce multiple stories of applying to higher education, beginning college, and transition. We learn about the hopes they have and how inclusive postsecondary experiences began to take shape.

Consider, for example, the excitement of adventure and the trepidation of the unknown articulated in some of these pieces. As students embark on their expanded lives, they share social, academic, and other barriers that they face in their quests for college. Students narrate the transition to college life and share the personal advocacy that was necessary for their inclusion. Through these pieces, they express and demonstrate that they deserve a space in university life and have much to both receive and contribute.

1

I Want to Go to College

Antonio E. Contreras

When I was a freshman in high school, I had to go to a high school where I would be in class only with other people like me who have disabilities. I wanted to be in classes with my friends from middle school. My mom met with the teachers and the principal of the high school to see if I could change my classes. They said no, and I was really sad and angry. Other kids made fun of us, and some of the kids bullied us. My mom got really mad, and she talked to the principal of another high school. I went to a different high school in my sophomore year where I could go to all the classes with everyone else. I also joined the basketball team and the cross-country team.

My Spanish class was in a classroom in the school library. There was a bulletin board outside the classroom where seniors posted the logos of the colleges where they were accepted. I was a sophomore, and I asked my friends if they were going to college, too. Everyone said they were going to college and they talked about what they wanted to be when they grew up. I wanted to go to college, too.

So, I went home and told my mom that I wanted to go to college just like my friends. She told me that maybe I could go to a community college, which is a college where you have to go to school near your house and live at home with your parents. She said that colleges where you go away and live there wouldn't accept me because I have an intellectual disability. I was sad and confused about that because I wanted to be like everyone else and go away to college and live there. Everyone was always telling my mom and me that I couldn't do things, but she advocated for me and sometimes she got mad and yelled at people so that I could do things like go to summer camp and go to basketball camps and be in classes with my friends.

My mom could see that I was sad. She googled "college for students with intellectual disabilities" and she found a list of colleges that have students just like me. Most of them were very far away. There were only two colleges in California, and I couldn't go to one of them because I had to be twenty-two years old. The other one in California wasn't good because we found out that all the students like me had to live together and go to class together. I wouldn't be able to live on campus or be in classes with other college students. I wanted to just be a student like everyone else.

My mom found two more colleges in Michigan where she has a lot of friends. We also found a college in another state where my dad has a lot of friends. We visited a lot of colleges. I applied to one college, and I was accepted! My mom was sad because the college was so far away and I had to take an airplane to get there, but I told her I was going to be okay. I went there for one year. My parents told me that I wouldn't go back for a second year. I can't talk about that, and all I can say is that all parties are satisfied.

At home I was sad and depressed and mad. I told my mom I didn't want to go to college anymore. I stayed in my room and played video games and watched a lot of YouTube and Netflix videos on my iPhone. My mom tried to make me happy by making my favorite foods, like acai bowls and mac 'n' cheese. My dad took me with him to go run errands with him. They gave me a lot of chores to do around the house. I got a gym membership so I could work out every day.

My mom told me I had to apply to college again. I told her I didn't want to go to college. That wasn't really true, but I was just upset. She told me I couldn't just stay in my room on my butt and

do nothing like the pirates who don't do anything in *Ve*
My parents helped me make goals so that I could focus
things that would help me get accepted to other col!
enrolled me in the local transition program so that I could have something to do during the day. I learned how to take the bus, wipe down tables at a restaurant, and fold clothes at a clothing store. I also took a basketball class at the community college.

My parents also helped me find a job. I found three jobs. I worked at the Amazon Fulfillment Center twenty-five hours a week scanning and loading boxes. I got paid $15.50 an hour. I had job support from the Arc San Francisco at Amazon. I met Congressman Ro Khanna and he offered me an internship in his Santa Clara office. Best Buddies helped me learn how to do my job at the congressman's office. I also got a summer internship at my church. I worked every day and I learned how to take Lyft to get to all my jobs and to school.

I started to feel better because I was learning new things and hanging out with people. I went to visit my friends from high school who went to college in California at UC Davis, Cal Poly San Luis Obispo, Stanford, and San José State. None of these colleges accepted students like me. So my mom looked again at the list of colleges that have students like me. She made a lot of phone calls and wrote a lot of emails. We made a list of nine more colleges all over the United States and we visited all of them. I am really good at finding my way around an airport. Also, my mom says that I am strong, and I carry her luggage when we travel.

My parents said that I had to apply to college, but it was my choice if I wanted to go or not. They said that if I didn't apply and I didn't get accepted, then I don't have any choices anyway. I filled out my applications. Some of them were late and past the deadline. I was very excited to be accepted to three colleges—Syracuse University in New York, Union University in Tennessee, and Georgia Tech. I liked Georgia Tech the best because the buildings and dorms and campus looked like San José State in California. Also, it doesn't snow in Georgia. The weather there is sometimes like California, but sometimes it's hotter and sometimes it rains more. My mom was sad again because Georgia Tech is far away from California, but I told her I would be okay. I am happy that my parents made me apply to college even though I told them I didn't want to go when I was sad. I'm glad because I had choices, and I really did want to go to college just like my friends.

Georgia Tech is so awesome. I have some classes that are only for students like me in the Excel Program and some classes where I am with students who are getting bachelor's degrees. Some of the classes are hard, and some are easy. I have a tutor that helps me with my homework. I also have a social mentor and a health and wellness mentor. I had an internship on campus at the Ferst Center where I took tickets and told people where they can sit. I go to football and basketball games. I joined a church group on campus. I also joined the public speaking club. My friend Erika and I decided to start a Best Buddies chapter at Georgia Tech. Erika is an engineering major and she is very smart. She was the president of her Best Buddies chapter at her high school in New York. I started a Best Buddies chapter at my high school with my friend Isabelle. Erika and I both had experience with Best Buddies. I went to the leadership conference at Indiana University six years in a row!

I had to go home before spring break in my first year because of the coronavirus. I made plans with my college friends Nick and Rashawn for spring break to visit my friend Chris Jones and his wife, Nanette, and their dog, Mochi. They live in Seattle but they used to live near me in California. I used to dog-sit their other dog, Yuki, when I was in middle school and high school, but Yuki died because he was old. After Seattle, my college friends and I were going to go to Los Angeles and go to Disneyland. But we all had to go home. I hope that we can go to Disneyland and Disney World after the coronavirus is over.

I am now in my second year of the four-year college program at Georgia Tech. I am taking four classes—Science Foundations of Health, the World Today, Financial Literacy, and Career

Success II. Some classes are virtual and some are in person. My favorite class is the World Today because I learn about history. The easiest class is the Science Foundations of Health class because I have to keep a workout log and I like learning about how to take care of my health. It is hard for me to understand some of my classes like Financial Literacy, but my tutors help me. Also, my dad is a special education teacher and if I call him, he will help me, too.

I have a job at L.A. Fitness where I open the gym on the weekends and I check people in and take their temperature. I have an off-campus internship as an office assistant at Decatur CoWorks. I have to take the MARTA train to Decatur and transfer from one train to another train. I have a campus internship at the Clough Undergraduate Learning Center information desk. When people have questions, I tell them where to go. I have three roommates. One of my roommates, Lee, is a biomedical engineering major, and my other two roommates, Nick and George, are in the Excel Program like me.

I like going to college because I am learning how to be independent. I can take Lyft by myself from home to the airport and take the plane to Atlanta, and I can take the MARTA train from the airport to the Midtown station and walk four blocks to my apartment. My mom helps me plan my meals every week with a spreadsheet. I use Instacart to order my groceries from Publix or Sprouts. I am learning how to make my own meals. I make my own chiropractor appointments and dentist appointments and flu shot appointments. I also make my own Covid-19 test appointments because we have to take a test every week. I take a screenshot of my test results and text it to my parents so that they don't worry about me. I am good at putting my appointments on my Google Calendar.

On Wednesday, November 4, 2020, I turned twenty-two years old. My house church group and my roommates celebrated my birthday with me. We had pizza and cookies. We had to eat outside because it's safer to eat outside than inside because of the coronavirus. We also wore masks when we were not eating, and I brought hand sanitizer so everyone could disinfect their hands. We had a lot of fun on my birthday.

A lot of people ask me if I miss my mom and dad and if I get homesick. I don't miss my parents that much. They visit me a lot, and they text me and we talk by video on my Facebook Portal. I told my mom that she had to stop texting me all the time. I told her she can only text me once a day. She looked sad when I told her that, but she understands that I need my space. When I tell her how I feel, she will change, even if it makes her sad. My mom misses me a lot, but she is also happy for me and proud of me because I am doing a good job going to college. My mom is always worried and that is annoying, but she is also awesome. I asked my dad to teach me how to drive when I go home for Thanksgiving and Christmas break, because I want to get my driver's license someday. My dad is awesome.

A lot of people ask me what I think makes a good college program. I think you need to have inclusive classes, not just classes only with students with intellectual disabilities. Also, it's good to have all kinds of friends and roommates and not just friends in the Excel Program. Also, parents should get on airplanes with their kids to visit colleges so they can see what the college is like before they go there.

I also like being at a college where there are a lot of different kinds of people. I am half Mexican American and half Filipino American. I have three roommates. One of them is half African American and half Filipino American, and the other two roommates are white. One of my classmates is from Switzerland. There are a lot of international students at Georgia Tech. One of my classmates was a foster kid for most of his life. I have classmates who are from all over Georgia and from other states. We are all different, and that's cool.

I don't know what I want to do after college yet. Next semester, I want to work at the airport as a wheelchair attendant. I am good at finding the gates at the airport and I like jobs where I am moving around. My trainer at the gym is a stuntman and an actor. He was in the movie *The Fate of the Furious.* I want to visit him when he makes a movie. My buddy Kyle works for the Atlanta Hawks of the NBA and I like basketball, so maybe he can help me get a job there. He also works for a photography and video studio where companies make commercials. I like acting, so maybe I can get a job there too and be in a commercial. I like to travel, so maybe I can work on a cruise ship or at a hotel. I know that I want to have a job so that I can pay for my own house, and someday I want to get married and have a wife and kids. I want to do what everyone else does and have a good and happy life.

2

I Got In

Taylor Ruppe

I was in my first period at high school, which was my cooking class, when I learned that I got into Appalachian State. I got called to the office. I thought that I was in trouble! When I got to the office, I picked up the phone, and my momma was on the phone. She told me I got into App State. I felt excited and happy that I got in. Once I got back to class, I told my teachers, and they were super proud of me because they knew how hard I had worked for this moment. Later that night, we celebrated my acceptance with a cookie cake saying that I got into App State, and my extended family sent me various things to celebrate my acceptance.

When I first got to App's campus, I was both nervous and excited. Trying to figure out where my classes were was a challenge. Luckily, my roommate was able to take me around campus before classes started to show me where my classes were. When we were going around campus, I took pictures of the room numbers to help me for the first day of classes. When walking around campus, I found that sometimes navigating the stairs could be a challenge. I work at the student union on campus. When I am at work, I clean up the tables that students use to study at; I also clean where people are putting their arms. This is especially important right now because of the coronavirus. At the end of my first year working in the student union, I won the lounge attendant of the year award. I was very happy after I received this award because I worked very hard for it throughout the year. I did my job to the best of my abilities.

3

Adventures in Postsecondary Education

Stirling Peebles

Students with intellectual and developmental disabilities should never give up on their dream of pursuing postsecondary education or transitioning to college. These students are totally capable of doing the hard and challenging work at college. I work at a postsecondary education program called Think College Vermont as their dissemination assistant. During my time at Think College Vermont, I have seen students with intellectual and developmental disabilities doing incredible things on a college campus.

As a student with an intellectual disability, I went through the graduation activities in 2001 with my class at Montpelier High School. However, I wasn't finished with high school yet. I did two additional years of schooling at the nearby vocational trade school. There I took computer networking and graphics communications with video production. I graduated in 2003. Therefore, the Individuals with Disabilities Education Act (IDEA) of 2004 didn't apply to me, so I never experienced the requirements that were laid out in the IDEA law. My transition planning in about 2001–2003 did not include postsecondary education, and I never really understood what transition planning could do for me. My parents were confused, too. We were new to the concept of transition planning and didn't know enough to fully engage. This planning started when I was a senior in high school, which was too late to help me plan my college goals. It should have started in middle school or earlier and should have been included in my Individualized Education Program plan throughout the years.

After high school, I knew I was ready for college. Although I did not matriculate at the Community College of Vermont, I took Foundations of Reading and Writing four different times. These foundation classes helped me to be successful at college writing and to have good reading comprehension at a college level. This played a major role in 2011 when I became a student at Think College Vermont at the University of Vermont (UVM). I always wanted to go to college because everyone in my family went to college. I too wanted to experience being a normal college student. In 2011, I applied and got accepted into the Think College Vermont Program at UVM, a two-year certificate program. I completed an eighteen-credit certificate with a concentration in film and media communications.

The Think College Vermont program gave me a chance to do something I always wanted to do. In this program I got to experience being on a college campus and made lasting friendships. I felt included and accepted in everything I did on campus and in the classrooms. While I was at UVM, I did a lot of observing and I felt accepted. The first few days I noticed peers were starting to accept me. At the same time, I felt like an outsider and wondered if they were going to like me as a person and not as a person with a disability. I learned so much on many different topics. I also learned how to study and do research. I was able to do something I never thought I could do, and now I can say I did it.

Going to college was challenging. It was hard work with a lot of homework, studying, writing, reading, and new experiences. Peer mentors provided academic and social support to students with intellectual and developmental disabilities at Think College Vermont. Mentors also helped students by being job supports for students at their internship sites. I took an interesting variety of courses and participated in two internships to fulfill the requirements of Think College.

I took a basic college writing class called Written Expressions in the fall semester in 2011. I wanted to be a better reader, to be able to think critically, and to write more effectively as a college student. The professor went over the syllabus for the class, and every student in class read a line out loud to everyone. I thought that was a fun way to start off the class. While in class, the professor handed out a student questionnaire and I filled it out. Everyone had to share a few things about themselves to the other students. I felt brave enough to share my personal information about myself, and I felt good about it.

After class, I walked over to the Waterman Café, and it was a nice place to hang out to have a snack. My peer mentor and I debriefed about how the class went, and we also discussed the questionnaire I filled out. Later in the day I took the campus bus to the Patrick Gym because I was taking a yoga class, and I thought it was fun. I took a yoga class for forty-five minutes, and I enjoyed the class. My first day at UVM was scary and exciting. I was looking forward to an interesting adventure. My final grade for Written Expressions was a B+.

On the last day of the semester, I went to my Written Expressions class without my mentor because I had the confidence to attend the class independently. At the end of the class, I handed in my final writing portfolio to my English professor, and that felt like a great accomplishment.

I took a class called Introduction to Poetry in the fall semester in 2012. I learned how to analyze poems, how to write haiku. I also learned a lot about different types of poetry. The class was fun, but it was extremely tough. I didn't realize this course would be so academically rigorous.

I took the class independently without a mentor from a third of the way through the semester, and I made new friends in class. I worked on a group project on Langston Hughes. In the group project, we incorporated a wonderful YouTube video spotlighting Hughes reading his own poetry. My favorite poets are Robert

Frost and Sylvia Plath. I did another analytical research paper on two poems by Sylvia Plath. I spent many hours in the library and utilized the undergraduate writing center. During my time in this poetry course, I analyzed poems and completed a research paper on Robert Frost. Writing the Robert Frost paper was difficult work.

I also wrote this original poem called "The Survival in the Woods."

The Survival in the Woods

Walking alone in the middle of the night in a strange woods.
All you can hear is spooky sounds from the animals within.
 You are too afraid of the sounds coming around you so you
 continue walking through dark, deep, creepy and spooky
 woods.
While walking around funny and strange looking trees brings
 an uneasy feeling to you because you can sense someone is
 watching you.
The deeper you go into the brushes it gets colder and the wind
 is picking up. A minute later, the clear icy water is falling
 down on your head and on the floor of the woods.
A second later, you can feel your feet soaking wet and bitterly
 frozen. Your entire body feels numb to the core, because
 you feel like you have been frostbitten.
As you continue walking in the frozen rain and the very cold
 blistering wind is making you pick up the pace, but your
 legs feel wobbly, shaky and hard to move.
A few moments later your legs give out and you collapse on the
 soaking wet floor of the woods. As you lay there all you can
 see is the pitch black sky.
Your body starts convulsing in a shaky way and there is nothing
 you can do about it and you feel hated and crazy angry that
 you didn't bring any layers with you on your walk.
All of a sudden you close your eyes and you fall asleep and the
 next morning you find yourself in a warm and cozy bed.
It was just a bad dream about survival.

I took my first college midterm exam during this class. This exam was exceptionally tough. It was a great learning experience. I received a B+ in this course.

I took a class called Introduction to Acting in the fall semester in 2013. On the first day of class, the instructor told us to get into a circle in the middle of the room, and we did yoga. In this class, I learned that acting is physical. I also learned how to do monologues and how to memorize a script. I made some wonderful friends in this course. I'm still friends with them on Facebook to this day. I received an A+ in this course.

I took a class on the development of motion pictures from its origins until the 1930s in the spring of 2013. I hoped this class would be interesting and fun, and it was. I learned about film theory and film history. The film screenings on Wednesday nights were a good opportunity to meet up with friends from my class. I learned a lot about silent films and enjoyed in-depth analysis of Charlie Chaplin's and Buster Keaton's films. It was a difficult class requiring a lot of reading and writing. Analyzing films was the most challenging part of this class. Group projects were also difficult because it was hard to coordinate everyone's schedule. My grade of B- reflected the challenges of this class.

Socializing and recreation at Think College Vermont were important aspects of my college experience. Attending Think College Vermont gave me the opportunity to meet many people and make many friends. I was thrilled when one of my friends would shout out at me from across the campus. When I was not doing homework, I enjoyed playing pool at the student center, and sometimes I won a few rounds. I spent many hours at the campus gym, and I enjoyed playing racquetball, doing Zumba, eating ice cream at free cone day, and using the punching bag.

Think College Vermont requires that each student participate in a semester-long vocational internship. I did my first vocational internship at a local news station in Burlington, Vermont. I was thrilled when I got this internship. On my first day at the news station, I felt nervous and scared, but this did not last long. I got to know the ropes of what to do and what not to do. I managed to learn my way around the studio. I was able to watch the news live from the set at noon, and I found that to be very exciting. Things only got better after the first day on the job. I went on location with the news team, I went on a commercial shoot with the advertising team, and I learned to edit video footage. I enjoyed working with professionals who know their stuff. In turn, I was able to share my knowledge and experience with these incredible people.

At the beginning of the internship, I had peer-mentor support, but eventually that faded out. I felt comfortable in the news station environment. This was a transition period for me because I was hoping to gain independence by taking a taxi alone to the job site. At first, I thought taking the taxi was scary, but then I started to feel comfortable. I had the same driver each week.

I also did a vocational internship at a local public access television station in Montpelier, Vermont. I had no peer-mentor support at this internship, and I did it independently. During this internship, I learned more about editing and camera work. I started working with a professional video camera.

In 2014, I graduated from the Think College Vermont program. This program pushed me to continue with higher education at Champlain College, where I earned a professional certificate in human resource management. My two years at Champlain College were completely remote. I missed the in-person engagement and being social with new friends. However, I became proficient in remote learning. This has helped me with my two jobs during the pandemic, as we all work remotely. My coursework at Champlain College helped me to become experienced in using the APA citation format. In 2019, I applied for and was awarded a nine-month graduate level fellowship at UVM in the Vermont Leadership Education in Neurodevelopmental Disabilities (LEND). The LEND program was a hybrid with remote and in-person classes.

As a person with an intellectual disability, I was given opportunities and chances to go to college and experience life on a college campus. I would never have gotten a meaningful job at the

University of Vermont without having participated in the Think College Vermont program. My video work with Green Mountain Self-Advocates was a direct result of what I learned from my internships.

All people with intellectual and developmental disabilities need to be given opportunities to have postsecondary education experiences that can lead them to meaningful employment in the community. The first step is to ask students with intellectual disability what they want to do in their future. Some students might want to be poets, artists, computer scientists, filmmakers, or game developers. Students with intellectual disabilities need to start thinking and learning about postsecondary education when they are in middle school. Special educators need to be talking about transition planning with students with intellectual disability and their families as early as possible. Attending college fairs and getting information about various programs can be helpful. Gathering support from family, friends, special educators, teachers, and instructional aides is very important. Transition planning helps plan for a person's future, including college education and employment. Transition planning must be based on a person-centered approach, and it also uses a family-centered approach. IQ is just a number. We want to be valued, respected, and meaningfully employed members of our communities just like everyone else. Postsecondary education can help achieve this.

4

A Language to Open

Adam Wolfond

I write a new language to open the way of thinking for different voices to be included. I am a nonspeaking man of autism who types and feels language moving like a dance of relation, thinking about the pace of the middle of it. Relation is key to education. My language is a call for the voices that walk and make new paths. I want to discuss the way I learn and that is the way of collaborative education at the A Collective, which is now renamed Disassembly (https://dis-assembly.ca). I have included my poems here to help understanding so that neurodiverse people can be included in education. One poem is a guide to the neurodivergent city, which applies to accessible education. My language leaks, is synesthetic, and saturates meaning. Will you dance with me?

Education has some good things and school is a different matter of people directing bad ways to control movement about the attention dancing still. Education is about accepting ways of artful contribution of ideas that are shared, having time to think about the ways of concepts and learning about them so we can shift them as we learn more about the world and about the way we need to help each other.

School is about the way control of knowledge is held by teachers and government. Easy learning opens doors, pacing the way of calm acceptance of doing things differently. The way of school does attention harm because the autistic attention is feeling and languages through the body that teachers say is disruptive, but the teachers disrupt the learning that is always happening, and we need good understanding about the way we see and feel each and every thing.

Education is the same when we think that people are all of the same way of thinking and perceiving; the real difference is that neurodiverse people are sensitive to lots of different things. Pace of the always-talking teachers and students is too fast so that I can't type as quickly, and I think fast so it is frustrating when people talk over me. I am perceiving at such speed it is overwhelming at times and I can't offer separated words at the slow language pace. I am not a slow-paced thinker. There is a difference between a fast-talking pace and how meaning becomes simplified, which I call slow-paced language because the action of thinking and feeling packs happening all at once. Thinking is always fast in speed and typing about it eddies like water pools and I am thinking faster like rain. I need the feeling of gravity to be settled; support manages the way of typing slowly. Managing the expectation of wanting teachers is pacing actual language and not virtual in the way that thinking and not writing happens. The virtual is the possible. So expression in proper afterthought of language is hard when teachers ask for articulate words that pack meaning into simple explanation. I perceive all at once so I manage by moving my body or holding objects, but the way people see me, the way of leering people, makes me anxious. Then my body moves fast. Good support is key to be settled and also allowing for my body to move. Good support also allows for artful ways of expressing.

I think room of managing a diverse classroom needs the understanding that people are not the same and this can open the pace to sound lining amazing band of jamming bodies and thoughts, questioning the way that school sounds like marching bands and not the jazz of improvisation. I manage magistrate, of doing school, like a falling trombone of bass dropping the sound to play sadness. Actual improvisation is the way of multiple sounds that jump and jive and can sometimes be like a groovy mess of meaningful languaging in the slappy ways of bodies pacing in different rhythms. Slapping is the way of nonviolence in my use of it, of body pacing in body, from one to many; I am good at thinking and that I am slappy like a happy dance.

Think about the middle of relation. The assembly is the collaboration of the middle, of feeling; it is the coming together, the engineering of each edge of existence to pace the pattern teaching us how the relation is always moving. I think that we are, at Disassembly, always of the band in walking together toward laughs and good tools for not sadness but joy. Reading is good to learn about other kinds of people who can join the assembly of tools for some rocking diversity. The way I am easy with learning uses aggregate of the way individuals are always a *room of many* and we are the future that is always good; for thinking about others as together and about diverse needs and wants traveling, needing more people and different ways of thinking. I think that I face the room; jamming the thoughts together is always the rock and roll of love. Real love is autistic attention dancing and feeling actual sensory reasoning about your way of thinking, but I want to bring answers buttressing the way of love-words to soon feel the calm way of being without the language of talking. Jam with me?

People Who May

May talking be questions
of managing important answers

May the people always want
autistics like me

May in the future we all
want each other

May the leaky language
of love bring in the walk
of dancing together

May the sound language
good easy expression

Maythetouchofhands
palmtogether

Mayeasytasteofcolors
illustrate leaky pace
of language and thinking

May the scent of talking
together always have openair

Maythetalkingsearch
forpeoplewhocare

OfWritingAboutFeelingandCumulativeFact

I am going to think about the way of academia
and the way we are supposed to write

I think that I can write racing thinking well
and I am wanting the way of writing
to actual feelings italicize the way
the world faces the pace party

Yes pace party is the way I am laughing
at the dance paving the ways
the words dance

The academy is the serious not
wanting fun of the way the laughter
family of thinking feeling rally lavishes
with love and really we should think
about the ways of desiring
not the ways of measuring people
about going to acting the way
easy people should

I am thinking thankfully at the way
we do things at the A Collective
and talking about ball I always think
needs to unravel questions
about thinking and perceiving
and the way we butter the human
as easy and the same

We need the way the world works
by assembling and disassembling
and the way we do that is by doing
and thinking and playing and saying
that of the way we assemble the movement
of writing about feeling and cumulative fact
of the aggregate experiments in art

Have the wanting academics an idea
pacing the way of real rallying experiments
without a goal of controlling the management
and outcome?

I think that the way actual face of relation
works has to have game of chance
and the camp in the way the people
can stay with each other in difference
and the way fragments variety sacrifice
the bossy sameness of what academy
seems to expect

The thanking audience of the rare
dappers the questions about the wanting future
of writing and the easy future for neurodiversity

The ways of dancing
the way of neurodiversity
is not the same rally
as academic critique

and we need pace
of accumulating steps
of wording walks pacing
movement with the ways
of wanting objects
and inspirations

The way of the sawing
wanting dance invites
paces will talking people
thank open thinking
about the possibilities?

My guide for someone to discover the neurodivergent city:

I would calmly tell
the story about being
timed pace

of the easy engineered amazing talker
without speech and the way the city
smells a meaningful tongue of
additive salty ram book of

autistic and sensory rally
landing the answers about
good neurodiverse city

The objects are calling me
to them as the way we are
languaging the wanting movement
and idea of the calm feeling is the waters

landing making less ran
love to the same place
of trees and terrific feeling

Bring the safe good typing to the neurodiverse city
Bring the good support of having good facilitators

I am also a facilitator of basic understanding
of different easy ways
of patterning and pasturing
and thinking with the earth

I am good at knowing about the facilitation
and watching the way
measures are in in in place
of how independence is
about the person and not
about the people

I am good at relating to objects in movement
and walking the city
of moving parts is flaneur
of neurodiversity

Game in in in the ways of human superiority
offers us little to manage
with and I am baffled
by the easy invested game
of humanity

5

"The Wanderer" and "This Is What I Sing"

Steven Brief

The Wanderer

My morals were strong
But my faith was waning
Waning like trees in a tough wind
My time passes
Like fish in a fast-flowing river
My mind is spinning
Like the leaves before my face
And yet I travel
No matter what obstacle
Whether blizzard, people or walls
I travel on
I leave bad impressions on the people I meet
Wherever I'm heading I don't know
Nobody knows
But I travel here and there
Never finding my place
Like a tree among shrubs
Like a sheep among wolves
Like snow in the summer
And a swimmer in winter
I stick out and I'm unlike the rest
So I put on a mask

White, plain and without distaste
Without emotion in truth
For behind the mask is a monster
At present all I can do is travel
But now my mind is clear
I'm truly running and not traveling
Cunning myself from what I can do
For the side of me that must stay hidden
Can't be hidden
I stop then and there and head to the nearest village
And walked among them
I tore off my mask
And among the gasps
One soul so tiny
Felt pity
The child took me in
Loved me
Cared for me
And I felt at home
Soon people saw the man I can become
And I became that man
For to leave the monster behind
I had learned the truth
And now I, the traveling monster
Had a story to tell
To tell my children my song
About the monster of a man
I point at the mask
The one I hung on the wall
And told my children my song
About the monster who took off his mask
And they'll ask how I changed
And I say I believed I can become
And I finally found peace

This Is What I Sing

As I walk slowly I began to see
That people are different than me
I sing my song
They think is wrong
I stick out this is what I sing
I do things so different
I see through eyes so different
I sing my song, they correct it
They sing a different song
So I duck and dive through the throng
Of people who say I'm wrong
But I sing a different song
All my life I sing differently
Do it differently
Talk, live and breathe differently
They speak of normal
What is normal I ask
Not you they reply so
I'm slower at one thing and faster at others
I wish I could like any other
Someone other than me
But I can't
So I struggle through life
Through happiness through strife
I sing my song differently
Maybe I'm wrong
Or maybe I'm right
Others are wrong
And now I sing a different song
One that's happy
And now not for long
Someday my song will be accepted and no longer wrong
This is my hope my prayers my song

6

My History of the Excel Program

Alex Smith

Have you ever felt like you were not going to be able to go to college? That's what I felt like at some points in my early life. During my childhood, I was behind on some parts of education as I was homeschooled and later went to a small private school. I felt like I was only able to learn at my own pace. Later on, in my teen years, I ended up starting at a public high school where I started hearing from some people about college programs for students that had intellectual disability. With only a year left before graduating high school, I began looking into and touring a couple of colleges around metro Atlanta. One of the colleges I found the most interesting was Georgia Tech, despite the fact that my parents and a couple of extended family members were University of Georgia graduates. Georgia Tech had some campus amenities that really amazed me, along with the fact that it has so much around it being in Midtown Atlanta. A couple of years prior, the Excel Program was established at Georgia Tech and was looking to grow.

After having successful interviews with a couple of colleges and getting accepted, the Georgia Tech Excel Program was my choice of where to have a college experience. I graduated high school in May of 2017, just before my twentieth birthday. In August of that year, I moved into a high-rise apartment in Midtown, next door to the Georgia Tech campus. During my first year, I spent my time exploring types of careers I would like, experienced living with roommates, took Excel classes on topics that I enjoy, went on some social outings, and explored campus clubs where I got to meet and get to know people. During the last half of my first year, I got my first on-campus internship as a tour guide around Georgia Tech's campus. I achieved this internship with my amazing skills on maps, directions to show people around who were looking to come to Georgia Tech, and researching about the campus with its history and facts. I decided to continue the internship the following semester due to me and everyone around me enjoying the tours. The other Georgia Tech tour guide students were really nice to me, and the Georgia Tech topics we discussed were interesting.

After my successful first year, I returned for my second year where I was having even more success. I began hosting a lot more social events of my own, such as having dinner outings and watching movies with my group of friends. During the first semester, I was successfully doing at least two Georgia Tech tours a week and improving on my tour guide knowledge, and it led me to look into what other internships I could do off of campus. My second year also had me in a very large American history inclusive class, something that I would have been scared about being a part of in high school. In the American history class, we learned and went in depth with things in history after the year 1877. Later in the following half of my year, I tried a couple more unique inclusive classes such as a civil rights class and one about the development of cities, called History of Urban Form. Later on, I finally got my first off-campus internship as an airport volunteer to help direct guests where to go in the terminal. It was nice but was also a challenge when trying to be trained on how to work, and it also led me to help out with a couple of things at the then newly renovated Georgia Tech Library. After my second year, I was at the halfway point where I got the first of the two certificates that Excel provides, which was for academic enrichment, social fluency, and career explorations. After this, I felt like

I completed a section in my college experience and was ready to grow for the following year.

I began my third year with taking inclusive classes and Excel classes about things that are useful for my adult life and future jobs, such as an organizational behavior business class, a financial literacy class, and the PEERS curriculum. Most notable for my third year was that I got the opportunity for an internship with the City of Atlanta. I went to the city hall and I would do something I enjoy, which was with maps on special software technology called geographic information systems. I learned how to use the software, despite that it was sometimes challenging. I worked through the challenge after doing some tutorials and my supervisors and coworkers showed me what I could do. After that special experience, I decided for the next semester to try another career field that was interesting to me, which was working with travel and hospitality at a hotel. I got an internship at one of Georgia Tech's nearby hotels, a Hampton Inn, where I got to help customers or assist with sorting and folding laundry. Things were going really well for me in the Excel Program, but something would cause a little downfall with the ending of my third year. That was the Covid-19 pandemic, which in March of 2020 shut down tons of places and canceled a lot of planned social events. Despite the sudden change, I would find ways that I can still prepare me for my final year in Excel.

I go into my fourth year and final year of Excel with some things more different than ever. Despite this, I worked hard to keep myself flexible. I returned to having my internship with the Hampton Inn after the people there wished to have me back. I also began learning about lots of things to help for postcollege time, as well as where I would like to have future jobs. For my final semester, I plan on finishing my required Excel classes and getting a job that I can have for after I graduate. I'm currently looking into having a job in Alpharetta where I'm from, which would either be at the YMCA front desk in Alpharetta or a hotel.

It's been an amazing opportunity for me to join the Excel Program. I'm really proud that I got a full college experience and learned so much along the way. I would like to thank all of the people who helped and supported me in the Excel Program and got me to where I needed to be.

7

Taking the Llama for a Walk and Other Things That Helped Us

Olivia Baist and Kylie Walter

Hi, I'm Olivia Baist! Hello, I'm Kylie Walter! We were the dynamic duo of Flint Hall at Syracuse University during the 2018–19 academic year. During that year, Olivia was a first-year student in the InclusiveU program, studying studio arts. Kylie was a junior and residential mentor for InclusiveU, studying inclusive education. We lived together as roommates, as well as friends, dancing and (mediocre) singing partners, gym buddies, study buddies, and co-filmmakers. Having similar and different interests and priorities is part of what makes the friendship worthwhile. For mentorships and roommate-ships, those differences can make things tricky . . . but we'll get to that later. Just so you have an idea of who we each are, we've listed some things and concepts that are important to each of us.

Now, Kylie is a first-year (graduate) student and Olivia is a junior. Older and oh-so-much wiser (kidding), we're here to share some of our perspectives and experiences from living together.

Meeting Each Other

And I was excited to meet everybody.
My mom and I were driving to Syracuse University.
We drove to Flint parking lot
Sometimes getting lost in circles!

Olivia's Positive Words	Kylie's Positive Words
Happy, Fantastic, Awesome	Family
My Bed	Friends
iPad and Phone	Coffee
FaceTime / Messenger / Texting	Learning and Studying
Word Searches and Coloring Pictures and Videos	Running
Walks	Reading
My Mom and Family	Jokes
Poems	NPR Podcasts
Friends	Music
My Boyfriend	My Bed
Dancing, Singing, and Music	Cities
Dance Shows / Musicals	Parks
InclusiveU	Photography
Syracuse University / College	Chocolate
Coffee and Water	Together
Together	

Figure 7.1. Olivia's and Kylie's positive words

ID, key, new water bottles in the lobby.
Up the elevator 1, 2, 3, 4.
Knock, knock, knock on the door,
"It's me, your college roommate!"

My mom and the new team moved my things.
We took the big bin back up the elevator,
And all needed lots of water.

A little nervous, but really happy.
I was so excited to be a college student
At Syracuse University and InclusiveU.
I said "this will be so much fun."

—Olivia

Dorm Room

Our dorm room was in Flint Hall, a residential building on campus mostly for first-year students. Flint was a welcoming space, made even better with an attached dining hall, mini-grocery store, study spaces, community lounges, and renovated bathrooms. Our floor was especially awesome, since we lived with the Education Learning Community. We were surrounded by a friendly, creative, and inclusive group that both of us "clicked" with. Olivia especially loved living in Flint, since there were so many opportunities there to meet and hang out with other first-year students. Kylie admits that though living in Flint brought back nostalgia from her own freshman year, socially, she would have preferred to be in a dorm with a range of ages and class years.

As visual people, our room in Flint was covered in decorations and constantly going through updates. Admittedly, the room as a whole was definitely a lot to look at. The back of our door was mostly reserved for reminders. We taped up everything from reminders for fire drill steps and weekly to-do lists to keep the room clean to lists of ideas for relaxing. As time moved on, our reminders overflowed to the sides of our closets or desks. Some of those reminders (we admit) came out of disagreements and bad days. For the most part, they were designed and created preemptively to make life easier and to test out new supports or ways of doing things. But the walls . . . oh, the walls! The walls were reserved for pictures of friends, cards, silly notes, and artwork. Since we collaged our walls together, we embraced those beautifully chaotic walls. Our room became our pride and joy. Our room was the one space on campus that *we* had complete control over, so it needed to be 100 percent our own and 100 percent for us. When we got home after a long day, we would look around at our safe-space creation, take a deep breath, and smile.

As all college dorm rooms are, our room was periodically checked by RAs and the fire department. Pretty much every time, we unfortunately were "fire-coded" and had to take some of our

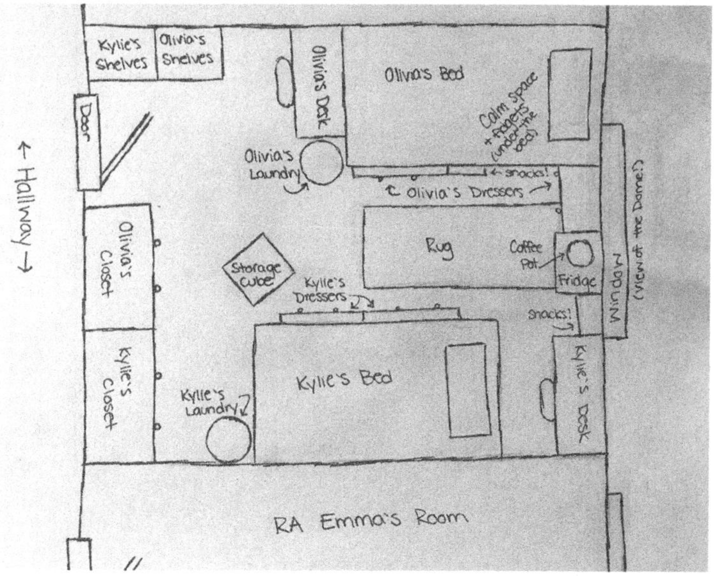

Figure 7.2. Map of Olivia and Kylie's dorm room. To the left of the door are their shelves, Olivia's desk, dressers, a drawer for snacks, and, under Olivia's raised bed, "Calm Space." To the right of the door are Olivia's and Kylie's closets and Kylie's raised bed with dressers underneath. In the middle of the room is a storage cube, rug, fridge, coffee pot, bin for fidgets, and drawers for snacks. A large window is opposite the door. Next door on the right is "RA Emma's Room."

reminders and artwork off the wall. Somehow more artwork always seemed to mysteriously appear back on our walls.

Camera

In October, we decided to start a video blog (or vlog). The vlog started as a fun thing to do together. We would film funny videos, dance around the room, and text them to each other as little pick-me-ups. The vlog quickly became more prevalent when Kylie asked to use some of the vlogs for her thesis project on inclusive peer mentorship on college campuses. After long conversations

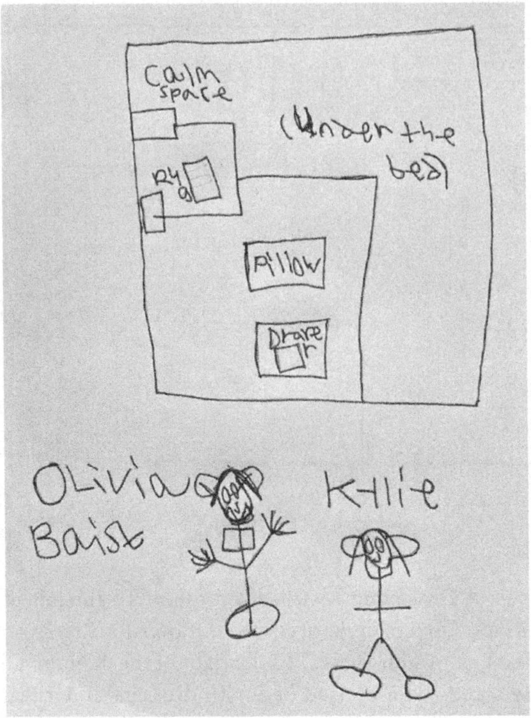

Figure 7.3. Olivia and Kylie's dorm room calm space. Olivia and Kylie are sketched at the bottom of the page. A rectangle in the middle shows the "calm space" under Olivia's bed. The bed is raised a few feet so that both Olivia and Kylie can sit under it comfortably without their heads touching the bed frame. Under the bed is a rug, a pillow, a set of drawers, and a small dresser. Not pictured in the drawer are fidgets, coloring books, and puzzle books.

about privacy, what might come from sharing our vlogs widely, and what the written portion of Kylie's thesis might say, we came to an agreement. We agreed to adopt Camera.

> We embraced this project to the point that "Camera" became our adopted third roommate, an embodiment of our dedication to sharing our experience.
>
> Recording as much as we did helped Olivia and I feel comfortable around the camera—rather, Camera. We grew to

Figure 7.4. Twelve different charts/visuals are posted on Olivia and Kylie's dorm room door. One chart is titled "When Kylie is not here or is doing homework" and eighteen options are written on colored paper squares, including "text a friend," "take a nap," "go for a walk," and "listen to music." Two smaller sticky notes indicate selected choices. Above the door handle is a reminder with a pink heart drawn next to it: "Remember: Key, Phone, ID." Another chart lists dates Kylie will be "teaching," "on campus," "home," or on "Spring Break!"

> not pretend or act when Camera was in the room with us; we grew to accept and embrace the idea that this project would be an honest portrayal of our experiences and who we were. If Camera was only allowed into our lives when we were dancing happily, this project would be a cute interpretation of college life. My intention was not to be cute.
>
> Camera was an incredibly helpful roommate, providing me with a way to deeply reflect. I was able to grow as a person, roommate, friend, mentor, and educator because of Camera. But sometimes, I wished Camera would go away. I wanted to kick Camera out of the room and call them a terrible roommate. Filming my life for almost seven months was hard. There were certainly days where I did not want to film.
>
> The truth is, Olivia and I did not film every second of our lives. Doing so would have been impossible for my hard-drive budget and too painful for our project mentality. This was an eight month-long project after all.
>
> . . . We worked hard to find a balance between dedicating ourselves to this project and making sure it did not become something we dreaded or saw as an invasion of privacy. Sometimes that meant kicking Camera out of our lives for a couple days. That was okay. (Excerpt from Kylie's May 2020 Senior Thesis)

It's because of Camera that we were able to make a film about our experience and share it with other college roommates, mentors and mentees, and friends. We're proud of how the film turned out and how we made sure it was a collaborative project from start to finish. It's also because of Camera that we can deeply reflect and reminisce now. Camera reminds us of our time as roommates, both the good and the . . . not so good.

Homework (Film Reference: 22:18–28:30)

Homework is something that all college students have. There are assignments outside of class and studying to be done in order to get the most out of college courses. How each student learns, works, and studies is different. This is an area where we, Olivia and Kylie, had our differences. Homework time was really hard for us, hard to the point where the word *homework* itself became a source of stress. For Kylie, homework time meant independent focus on assignments and readings with her laptop out and headphones on. For Olivia, homework time meant having to sit alone, be quiet, and not having wanted (or needed) social interactions. It was a time when our needs clashed—often resulting in tears, arguments, and cracks in our relationship. To make things a little more humorous, but to still be able to have productive conversations about study times, we dubbed "homework" "taking the llama for a walk." Weird and silly, sure. But it helped us.

When do my needs get to come first
In a situation where I agreed to put myself second?
When do I get to be a student
In a situation where being a student hurts my friend?

I want to sit at my desk.
Coffee hot. Sweatpants on. Music playing. Homework out.
I want to read, to write, to learn—
To do the very thing I came to college to do.
I just need to be just a student.
Just for a little bit.

But if my need brings my best friend to cry,
Brings my roommate to feel so alone
Lost and in fear of being forgotten,
Brings words to cut us so deep
That we both bleed,
Brings guilt to cover me at night instead of sheets,
How can my need even be a need at all?

—Kylie (Edited, April 2019)

During homework time I felt . . .	Because . . .
Frustrated	**Olivia** → Mad. Sad. I would rather be doing something with Kylie. Sometimes Kylie wanting space would make me frustrated because it was not what I needed. I needed help feeling calm after I felt frustrated.
	Kylie → Sometimes I felt like I was not allowed to do work or be a student myself. It felt as though my own academic needs were not valued.
Tired/Exhausted	**Olivia** → I was bored and did not want to do anything else and it was late at night.
	Kylie → It was exhausting to sometimes have to wait for Olivia to fall asleep to start my homework. Doing something that I knew would upset both of us was mentally draining.
Shame	**Olivia** → And I felt a painful emotion because I felt bad. I was feeling sad and mad because I needed attention. Sometimes I would tap Kylie twice for attention and stand close to Kylie's desk to be distracting. I was not good.
	Kylie → Doing homework felt selfish. I felt like a terrible friend for repeatedly causing this same conflict almost every night. My struggle to balance supporting Olivia and supporting my own academic growth brought me to feel inadequate.
Lonely	**Olivia** → I was doing lots of things on my own for a long time. I would feel upset and want to talk to friends, but they were busy too.
	Kylie → In the moments of homework-related conflicts, I sometimes felt like no one was there for me or to listen to what I needed.
Calm	**Olivia** → And I like to do things like coloring, music, reading, sudoku, crosswords, word search, watching shows, dancing, typing paragraphs, and taking relaxing showers. This is what I did when Kylie was taking the llama for a walk.
Motivated	**Kylie** → We had daily conversations about how we were going to make homework time better that always felt productive. We consistently worked together to make schedules and plan supports. We knew we could figure something out for both of us.

Figure 7.5. Kylie's and Olivia's feelings during homework time

Homework (or . . . the need to take the llama for a walk) was not going away and couldn't be ignored. So, we had to figure out a way to make it work for both of us. Over the course of the year, we realized that there was not just one way to make homework time tolerable or productive. We had an index card next to Kylie's desk that would say "It's quiet time" on one side and "We can talk now" on the other. We had a list on the back of the door of quiet, relaxing choice activities to do when one of us was trying to focus independently. We made a "quiet space" underneath Olivia's raised bed, fixed with a fuzzy rug, large pillows, a weighted blanket, coloring books, headphones, cool lighting, and (of course) snacks. We had a whiteboard schedule that we wrote out together every day, planning when homework time would be and what we would do before and after. We had a bag of fidgets, coloring books, and sudoku puzzles that we would bring with us pretty much everywhere. We rewarded ourselves for taking the llama for a walk by taking walking breaks or getting coffee together.

Sometimes, we took homework time out of the dorm room. We would go to the lobby of our dorm building, take over empty classrooms on campus, or find two spots relatively close together in the library. Together, we established a different routine and set of supports we would each use individually depending on where we chose to have quiet time. We found that changing the location of homework frequently helped us to not associate a certain place with bad experiences. We also found that we were too good of friends and too attached for our own good. Doing homework or quiet time in the same spot made individual, distraction-free focus really hard.

On particularly hard weeknights, Kylie would go to the library alone to do homework and Olivia would hang out in Flint. Typically, Olivia would see if a friend on the floor or an RA would be free to hang out. A few RAs would welcome Olivia to help them with their RA duties at the front desk. Other times, Olivia would just try to relax and chill in the dorm room until Kylie came home. Sometimes these strategies worked for us. Sometimes they did not.

Figure 7.6. Taking the llama for a walk in the classroom. Hand-drawn sketch of what homework might look like for Kylie and Olivia if studying in an academic building. The top of the sketch is labeled "Classroom Academic." There are multiple desks and chairs, a projector screen, two charts hanging on the walls, and a door of a classroom. Olivia is drawn sitting near a drawer in the back of the room. Kylie is not drawn in this picture (and is presumably in a similar setup in a nearby empty classroom).

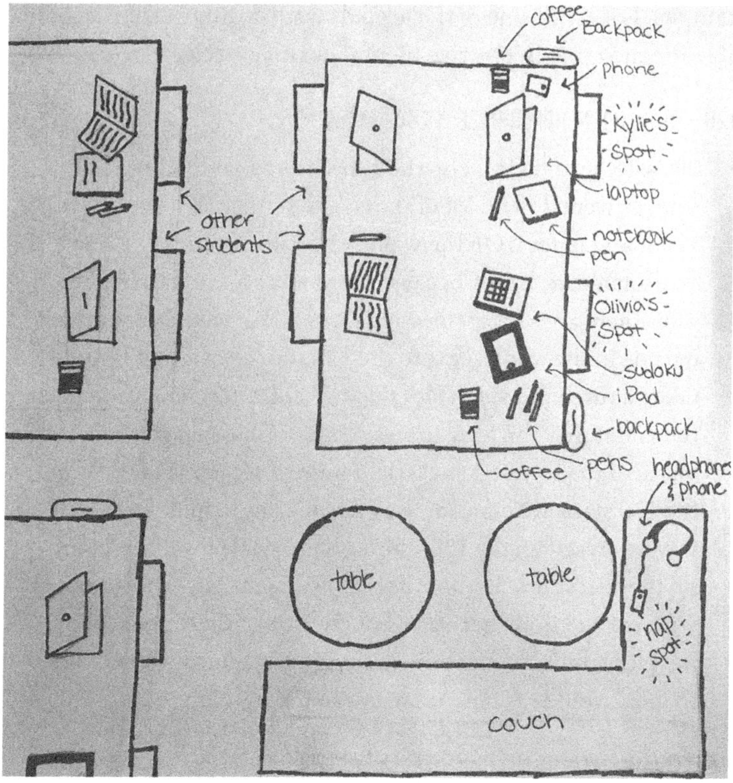

Figure 7.7. Taking the llama for a walk in the library. A map that imagines Olivia and Kylie's homework setup in the university library. Next to "Kylie's Spot" is a sketch of coffee, a laptop, notebook, pen, phone, and backpack. Beside Kylie's Spot is "Olivia's Spot," with a sketch of a sudoku book, iPad, backpack, pens, and coffee. Across the table are chairs for other students and simple sketches of their belongings. At the bottom of the map are two tables in front of an L-shaped couch with a "nap spot" nearest Olivia's spot, and a pair of headphones and phone that Olivia would often use.

Supporting Each Other

Homework was not the only thing we, as college students, had to work on. College is not just about classes! We both had individual long-term goals that we worked on together and individually. One of those goals for Olivia was independently traveling around campus. For Kylie, one of those goals was holding herself accountable for engaging in positive mental health practices.

120 STAIRS (FILM REFERENCE: 33:46–34:44)

Olivia: Kylie and I went on the 120 stairs to get to Flint Hall. And we went down a lot of stairs. The stairs were covered with a roof and fences. On the walls were lots of paintings. The stairs made me happy because there was a lot of walking outside. There are a lot of trees and flowers. We would see animals outside in the woods next to the 120 stairs. Kylie and I would take pictures and video blogs on the stairs. It is hard to walk on the 120 stairs. You have to wear comfortable sneakers or boots on the stairs so you do not trip. I wanted someone to walk up the 120 stairs with me in case I needed any help. It was a long way by myself on the 120 stairs. I had a goal of walking alone on the 120 stairs. It's not that easy because I need someone with me so I don't get scared or anything. There are a lot of people walking on the stairs talking and saying positive words to me. I would say positive words to them.

POSITIVE MENTAL (AND PHYSICAL) HEALTH PRACTICES

Kylie: Between classes, work, big projects, filming, and trying to be a good roommate, I was a busy person. I'm not proud of how I let healthy mental and physical health practices get pushed to the side. What I am proud of is that I recognized this early on and made a plan to help myself. Together, Olivia and I joined several classes for Syracuse University's Orange Pulse Dance Troupe. Having been a less-committed member of Orange Pulse the year before, I knew what I was getting into. This would be a way for me to have a few set times a week to physically drain myself and have some fun social interactions with friends and fellow dancers. I would be held accountable for my goal of staying physically and mentally healthy. Win-win.

Except . . . as much as I love to dance, I'm actually a terrible dancer. I have no coordination, flexibility, knowledge of technical moves, formal experience, or skills to keep up with choreography. I struggled to maintain the confidence to believe that giving a rehearsal 100 percent effort was worth it. In the back of my mind I knew that dancing would eventually feel like a 100 percent good thing. I just had to get over this initial bump and be confident. Thankfully, I had some wonderful friends (looking at you, Olivia) who were pros on the technical side of things and who were more than happy to review choreography with me. Over time, with a lot of practice and a LOT of help, I grew to feel better about dancing with the troupe. My technical skills never dramatically improved (that's okay), but my confidence did increase with practice. The more confident I felt, the more I enjoyed dancing with friends, the healthier I felt.

We also had mutual goals. One of those mutual goals was utilizing staying-calm strategies in high-stress situations, like fire drills (film reference: 14:44–16:01). We found that having a list of steps and communicating needs up front (like needing a hug) was helpful for both of us.

Olivia: The fire drill was so loud in my ears. Outside were fire trucks and ambulances. The ambulance lights and emergency lights were loud and bright. First step when the fire alarm goes off is to put shoes on, get our keys, phone, ID, and glasses. (During my junior year, I have to wear headphones and a mask for Covid-19 during fire drills.) We always have to turn the lights off and leave the room. Then we lock the door. We walk down stairs because you cannot go through the elevator. After that, you go across the driveway to get to the grass. Wait for the fire trucks and ambulance to come.

Sometimes, supporting each other and our mutual goals didn't have to be anything complicated. We would remind each other

Figure 7.8. Calming down in a classroom as roommates. A sketch shows Kylie and Olivia sitting at two chairs in an empty classroom. In front of them on the wall is a dolphin on a projector screen, a scene from the nature documentary that Olivia and Kylie were watching at this moment. Behind them are many unused chairs in the classroom.

to think of positive things when stressed or to count backward until we could think clearly again. It was also important for each of us to recognize our differences in what we each need to feel calm. For Kylie, quiet spaces, drinking tea, stretching, writing lists, and watching nature documentaries were some go-tos. For Olivia, seeing friends, talking to family, coloring, reading, listening to music (specifically pop music, country, and top hits), sudoku puzzles, showers, yoga, playing pool, and going to the gym were helpful.

College Life and Roommate Bonding

We both wanted to be college students first and foremost. That's why we're here. Through Camera, we have a lot of those moments, of us just being college students, caught on camera.

On Friday and Saturday nights when it was too cold (or we were feeling a little lazy), we would lay out blankets and gather our favorite junk food to enjoy relaxing movie nights. If we were feeling more social (which was usually the case), we would join friends for university-sponsored late-night recreation (Orange After Dark Events). Since we both love to dance, we joined the Orange Pulse Dance Troupe together and enjoyed practicing for the annual showcase with fellow dance and music lovers. Sometimes we wanted to go off on our own roommate adventures off-campus, just the two of us! We would go for walks in the park or around the city, take a bus to the mall, or play in the snow. Looking back, one of our favorite roommate trips was to Barnes & Noble (film reference: 9:21–10:31).

> **Olivia:** Kylie and I went on a Barnes and Noble trip. And Kylie was helping me to look at the books about romantic relationships. I wanted to learn about boyfriends and being a girlfriend. Kylie was looking for a biography to read for a class assignment. In the store I said, "Hey Kylie, do you want to help me look for a book with long chapters, big words, and some pictures?" We looked at the covers, titles, summaries, and a few pages to help each other find the perfect book. And this took a long time! We went in circles and sometimes went to the same section twice . . . or three . . . or four . . . or five . . . or six . . . or seven . . . or eight . . . or nine . . . or ten times! And I really liked helping Kylie choose and she helped me choose. We both had to make sure we had enough money in our budgets.

Not all of our roommate bonding or general college silliness involved leaving campus. Our fun didn't have to be super planned or structured! There were a million places on campus to explore, and we enjoyed walking around to find the coolest spots together. Sometimes, if we found a particularly cool spot, we would stake it out. Usually, Camera was not invited to these outings. There were a few exceptions (film reference: 34:49–36:09):

> **Kylie**: Olivia and I would frequently take over academic classrooms after hours. College classrooms are seriously underrated places to hang out! Classrooms with smartboards, a good sound system, swivel or rolling chairs are the jackpot. After we were sure students and professors had left for the night, we would take over and enjoy the freedom of having a large space to ourselves. One of the few times we let Camera join, we had picked up Insomnia Cookies before heading to Huntington Hall, played a variation of soccer in rolling chairs through the hallways and danced through every room and stairway to some classic throwbacks. It was *late* before either of us checked the time and realized we should head back to our dorm. Exhausted, we trekked through the snow and back up the 120 stairs.

The best thing about being roommates was also what made being roommates so hard. We were roommates and mentor/mentee first, but our relationship quickly became a friendship first and foremost. Having that genuine friendship was the best! We were able to talk about anything together, were always there for each other, and enjoyed each other's company. From Orange Pulse Dance classes, to campus events like OttoTHON, to university musicals and plays, to coffee trips, we were side by side, loving every minute. We felt like we could be ourselves around each other.

But at the same time, having all three of those pieces together (being roommates, friends, and in a mentorship), our relationship was really complicated. With the roles we played in our multi-dimensional relationships constantly switching, setting up boundaries was really challenging. We had to have some conversations as roommates that did not feel like a conversation among good friends. At times, our mentor/mentee relationship felt like it was stuck in the middle between being roommates and friends. Some of our talks about support were directly related to helping each other as roommates or college-student peers, while others directly related to helping each other as friends. Having other mentors and friends around was helpful at times. We both felt like it was healthy to spend time with other people and take a break from each other, no matter how hard it was to be apart.

After our time as roommates and mentor/mentee came to an end, all that remained was our friendship. In a way, our friendship is better now (two years later) because we don't have to go through the roommate arguments and homework-related conflicts anymore. At the same time, our friendship was stronger when we were roommates because we spent so much time together. We both agree that we'd take being roommates again any day! We miss living in Flint Hall, room 471 together.

We can't forget to tell you more about our film! We wanted our film to go beyond saying, "Inclusion works," to say, "This is *how* an aspect of inclusion can work." It's important to note that even though the film includes our thoughts and the thoughts from eleven of our peers, the film does not show all experiences or perspectives on mentorship. Student experiences and perspectives, whether represented in our film or not, are valid!

It was quite the experience being filmmakers and featured in the film!! The good thing about being the filmmakers was that we got to choose what was included in the final cut. But now that the film is out there, we don't know exactly who will see the film or how it will be interpreted by others. It's a little bit scary to be so vulnerable to people we won't know! We're not perfect people and didn't always get mentorship right. The film is honest about that fact. If the film only showed the good times, not much learning would come from it. We're glad that the film represents the whole big picture.

We started doing this work because we like working together. We're continuing to do this work because we are proud of the work we've already done. We want to share what we learned with future students in inclusive mentorships or in higher education so that they can start from where we finished. *And They Were Roommates: Navigating Inclusive Mentorship in Higher Education* is a film project by students, to students (and those who continue to support inclusive college opportunities for all students).

Part II

Opening Up Possibilities

OVERCOMING DOUBT AND UNCERTAINTY

"Opening Up Possibilities" represents the optimism of this generation of advocates. In this section, we collect stories of personal hardship, hopeful perseverance, and triumph over adversity. This idea of prevailing despite the discrimination of society and social structures is not one that is unique to students with intellectual disability, and many of the student voices shared here reflect intersectional identities pushing against pervasive prejudices.

The idea of actualization echoes throughout the pieces. How do students, most of whom would not have had access to higher education a decade ago, face the harsh realities that exclusive spaces present? This section has a cumulative effect, stacking experiences of resolute tenacity in a way that builds toward a common goal of full inclusion.

Allen Thomas's chapter title communicates volumes for all of the authors: "I Did What They Said I Couldn't."

8

Being Independent Has Risks

HOW TO RECOVER WHEN SOMETHING TERRIBLE HAPPENS

Kailin Kelderman, Eilish Kelderman, and Mary Bryant

Note: This essay discusses sexual assault.

Background Info

KAILIN

My name is Kailin Kelderman, but sometimes I go by KK. I am twenty-five years old and I live in my own place. I graduated from college a few years ago and I have Down syndrome. After high school, I didn't want to go to college. I got my dream job at Bully's Bar & Grill. I was a bus girl, but I could not understand some of the languages other people were speaking. It was hard for me. The next year I applied to college at the University of Nevada, Reno (UNR). My mom created a program called Path to Independence (P2I) for people with disabilities, like me, to go to college. I got accepted into the program and got a big scholarship from Ruby's Rainbow to help me pay for college.

When I started the Path to Independence program, I moved into a small house across from the university with my friend, Nancy. After a while, Nancy moved out and I had two roommates move in. My two roommates were Alexandra and Michaela, and they were in the program with me. We would sing together and talk to each other a lot. We would go to lunch together at the student union and eat Panda Express. Sometimes roommates don't get along, like when one of my roommates would eat my food. It's okay that roommates don't get along sometimes. We are all still friends and I had fun living with them.

I took a few different classes at UNR. My favorite class was my sociology class. There were other P2I students in my class and we had a good mentor. I got to do a report on Jonestown, and it was really interesting. I also liked my photography class, swimming lessons, and women's studies. During college, I also had a job at the student union information desk and helped people find different things on campus.

I graduated from college after two years in the Path to Independence program in 2017. I'm happy I went to college because I learned about different classes and had a good job. After I graduated, the landlord of my small house across from UNR sold my house, so I had to move out. I decided I wanted to live by myself, without roommates, and my aid helped me find a small studio apartment that was attached to the back of a different small house close to UNR. It was really small, but I liked being on my own and independent.

The job coach at the Path to Independence program helped me find my new dream job at Laughing Planet. I was a prep cook at Laughing Planet, and I walked to work by myself every day. I was always early and would get hot chocolate at the coffee shop next to Laughing Planet before my shift. I would make the best guacamole at work and got free lunch, too. My boss and coworkers were nice.

When the coronavirus started spreading in March of 2020, I lost my dream job at Laughing Planet. It was sad for me because I really liked working there. The house my studio apartment was attached to opened up and I moved in there with another P2I graduate. It was a big house with two bedrooms, one bathroom, and a really big living room area. When we moved in, I wanted my new roommate, Casey, to feel comfortable. I wanted to make the house less scary because Casey had never lived on her own before. I wanted to make her feel safe in the house with me.

MARY

I am KK's mom. I work at the Nevada Center for Excellence in Disabilities at the University of Nevada, Reno. I worked for several years to get the Path to Independence program started because I wanted Kailin to have a place to go to college. The program got started just as KK graduated from high school. Exercising her independence, she said, "I don't want to go to college." She worked for a year and then attended the P2I program the following year. She lived in a small house near campus with roommates. When the rental was sold, she moved into a tiny apartment by herself. When the larger two-bedroom unit opened up, she moved into it with another P2I graduate. In each of the different housing experiences, she did well, just making some of the same mistakes that we all did when we moved out, like getting locked out of her house. But she learned from every experience, and I've always been very proud of her independence.

EILISH

I'm Kailin's younger sister (her only and favorite sibling), and I'm currently in the midst of earning a master's degree in social work at the University of Nevada, Reno. I graduated with my undergraduate degree in political science and developmental disabilities in 2018. I've always been passionate about the disability community and interested in policy, so I hope to work on a macro social work level to implement inclusive and progressive policy for people with intellectual and developmental disabilities. Every obstacle Kailin's faced, she's been able to overcome. She went to college and graduated. She's lived on her own for several years (with and without roommates). She's had different jobs and learned a lot along the way. Kailin has always been a badass. She's an incredible young woman who thrives on her independence. I'm proud to call her my big sister, inspiration, and best friend.

When Something Bad Happens . . .

KAILIN

In May of 2020 I was raped by a guy named "David" (not his real name, but the name he gave me). I did not know him. He walked by my house that morning and came back that night and knocked on my window. He did something really bad to my phone. He took videos on my phone of the rape and asked me, "Was that fun?" He put his phone number in my phone and sent the videos to his phone. Then he left. He made me bleed a lot. He pulled my hair. When I saw the videos, I deleted them because I could not take it anymore.

I wasn't ready to tell anyone until the morning. I was trying to decide what the best thing to do was. I texted my mom at 7:30 a.m. the next morning and said, "A man had sex with me, and I could not stop him." My mom called me, and I told her that a man came into my house during the night and had sex with me. She came over right after we got off the phone. When my mom got to my house, my roommate and I sat at the table with her. I told my mom what happened, and we called the police. My mom called my dad and then called my sister, Eilish. Eilish was in tears when my mom told her what happened to me because she was scared; she almost lost her sister. My mom told me that it wasn't my fault and I know I didn't do anything wrong.

MARY

That 7:30 a.m. text was a mother's worst nightmare. The idea that someone would hurt her in that way, in any way, made me so angry I thought my head would explode on the eight-minute drive to her house. But I knew I had to calm down because I wanted to support KK, who had to be so hurt and confused. When I arrived, she was shaky and a little teary, but seemed okay. We sat down and she told me what had happened. Despite the trauma, she was able to remember a lot about the attack and she showed me things that would become evidence. She also told me that her attacker had videotaped the rape and sent it to her. As disturbing as that was, I knew it meant that he could be found. I felt so terrible for her. How could someone hurt her like that? As a mom, you want to protect your child and take away her pain, and I felt incredibly inept at both.

EILISH

My phone rang around 8 a.m. on May 6, 2020. I answered the phone, and my mom told me Kailin had been assaulted. It was the worst moment of my entire life. At first by "assaulted" I thought she meant Kailin had been mugged or beaten up by someone. My worst fear came to life when my mom said she was raped. There aren't words to describe that horrific feeling. I started crying. How could someone do this to her and take advantage of her like this? I asked my mom if I could talk to Kailin, and I told her I wouldn't cry when talking to KK. I asked KK, "How are you? Are you okay?" She responded hesitantly and with a shaky voice, "I am okay. He hurt me but I'm going to be okay. I told mom and the police are coming." I told her it wasn't her fault and that she didn't do anything wrong. Kailin said she wasn't ready to see my dad or me yet, so I drove over to my parents' house to see my dad while we waited for updates.

Aftermath: Interviews, Exams

KAILIN

My mom called the police and told them what happened. The police came to my house and asked me some questions. I told them about the videos. I gave them some evidence, like my underwear and the washcloth I used after. The police officer wanted to talk to my roommate, Casey, too. She didn't hear anything because it was late and she was in her room sleeping. Then the police officer talked to me about the forensic exam. He said they could get some DNA from the exam, and it would help find him and send him to jail, so I decided to do it. I want to make sure he doesn't do this to my roommate or other people.

We followed the officer to the place where I had to have the forensic exam done. I went into the forensic exam first and my mom waited outside. I wanted to go in by myself and do it on my own. After the nurse was done, they wanted me to take a lot of medicine so I wouldn't get different diseases or infections. They told me I would have to get a blood test in six weeks, six months, and in one year to make sure I am okay and don't get sick.

That night, Eilish took me to her house. We had pizza and chicken wings and watched my favorite movies. She got me comfort foods like popcorn, chips, and candy. Then I decided to stay with my parents for a while. A few days after everything happened, I moved my stuff back into my parents' house. I went back to the building where I had the exam done to have an interview. When I was interviewed, the police and other people were in a different room, and they recorded it so I didn't have to keep telling them what happened. They asked me a lot of questions, and I told them everything.

MARY

I had heard stories about how rape victims are sometimes treated, so I didn't know what to expect from the police. The officer who came was very kind and efficient. He spoke to Kailin like any other person and did not talk down to her, which I really appreciated. When she did not understand, she'd look at me and I'd explain it in a different way. For the trauma she'd been through, she was able to answer questions and give information to the officer.

The officer talked to KK and me about the forensic exam (rape kit). He explained that the best way to help in finding her attacker and sending him to prison was to have the forensic exam, where they could gather his DNA as evidence. But he told her it was her decision. She looked at me and my heart broke. I knew the right thing to do was for her to have the exam. But knowing how invasive it would be, especially after just being raped, made me want to take her and run. She asked if it was an exam like the Pap test (her first) she had recently had, and I told her it was similar. We talked about it, and she decided to have the exam. She really wanted to make sure he could not hurt anyone else.

When we got to the clinic, Kailin wanted to go in alone (as she did for her first Pap test). It surprised me, but I was glad she felt confident and trusted the women who were caring for her. When it was over, she had a ton of medicine to take and blood work to be done to check for STDs. We left there with information about counseling and the police routine that would follow. We were hooked up with the Washoe County Victims of Crime Program, which could pay for her relocation, counseling, and other services needed as a result of the rape. Now it was time to go home and digest all that had happened.

EILISH

My dad and I sat on the porch waiting for any texts or calls from my mom. The one thing that I had to keep reminding myself was that she was alive and was going to be okay . . . eventually. I got a text from my mom saying they would be going to get a forensic exam (rape kit) soon. The thought of her having to be violated, again, in that way broke my heart even more. Her innocence and privacy were completely stripped from her all within a matter of less than twelve hours. Why did this have to happen to her? She is the last person on this planet to deserve this.

I went to the store and bought a bunch of KK's favorite snacks and picked up lunch for everyone. When KK came home, I had never squeezed her so tight. Kailin has always been brave, but I could see it even more so now. She started talking about what happened. The heartbreak following those conversations was indescribable. I grew so angry with this pathetic excuse for a human being who did this.

KK and I had previously made plans to hang out that night anyway, but I didn't know if she was still going to be up for it. I was surprised and happy when she said, "I get to go over to Eilish's house for pizza and movies tonight." I wanted to spend as much time as I could with KK. I never wanted to let her go. We ordered pizza from our favorite local spot, Nu Yalk Pizza, and we watched her favorite musicals to sing along to: *Mamma Mia!* and *Frozen.* There were some moments I would see her looking off and tearing up, then she would go back to singing along. I had to excuse myself a few times to stop myself from crying in front of her. Seeing her able to sing and laugh along to her favorite movies gave me some sense of reassurance that she was going to be okay and able to recover from this.

Waiting Game

KAILIN

The weekend after I was raped, I decided to move out of my house and moved in with my parents. My family and friends helped me move all of my stuff. I didn't want to live in that house anymore. I wanted to live with my parents to recover and get my justice back. I was kind of sad after the rape, and I think I had some anxiety. My mom's coworker and friend, Denise, brought me cupcakes and talked to me about everything. She had also been raped when she was younger. She told me it was not my fault and that I didn't do anything wrong. Other people came over and brought me stuff, and I got sent flowers, too.

MARY

The waiting was hard. KK moved back in with us. She seemed okay but quieter and more reserved than usual. We were waiting for the Reno Police Department to assign a detective to the case, which took about a week.

KK had told us that she met her attacker earlier on the day it happened, when he was walking a dog down her street. Eilish and I figured that most people walk their dogs on a pretty regular schedule. So, while waiting for the police to assign a detective, we decided to stake out the house. We wanted to do something instead of just waiting. We got up really early in the morning and parked a half block from the house, where we could see anyone walking by her house. Our plan was to follow him so we could tell the police where he lived. Of course, Nancy Drew and her mom had no luck. We would find out later that he was walking a friend's dog and he did not live in the neighborhood.

About a week after the attack, we got a call from the detective assigned to the case. Kailin went back to the Advocacy Center, where she was interviewed by a forensic interviewer. The detective, assistant district attorney (DA), and others assigned to KK's case were in another room listening. It was explained to me that this way, if any of them had other questions, they could have the interviewer ask them right away. It's also done this way so that KK would only have to tell the story one time, instead of numerous times to different people. I appreciated that.

EILISH

The days following the attack were really hard. I was at my parents' house visiting KK every day. I had no appetite. I could hardly sleep, and when I did, I had awful nightmares. It was all I could think about. I kept telling myself that I would feel better once he was caught. I kept learning smaller, but heartbreaking, details about the assault as the days passed. Waiting for any form of information was so hard. I felt helpless. We couldn't get a hold of our victim advocate and had to wait to get a detective assigned to our case. In the meantime, my mom and I decided to stake out KK's old house to see if we saw anyone matching the assailant's description. Not surprisingly, we didn't have any luck. What we did discover in the meantime was that we could go into our family phone plan to find the number that had sent KK the horrific videos she deleted. Later on that day, I took the phone number and paid for several different website search engines to search the phone number. I didn't know it at the time, but the phone number was registered to her assailant's ex-wife.

About a week later, our assigned detective called me. I gave him the information I found, and he said he would contact my mom and Kailin next to schedule a forensic interview. Kailin met with a forensic interviewer while the DA, detective, and others on KK's case watched in another room. They did this so that she didn't have to repeat her story over and over again. My family and I were really grateful for that.

Arrest and Bail Hearing

KAILIN

After a few weeks, my mom told me that our detective called her to tell us they found him and arrested him. I asked our district attorney to explain to me about what was going to happen with the court. We had to go to a bail hearing on Zoom because of the coronavirus. The DA told me I could write something for him to read at the bail hearing to the judge. I told him I feel frozen, and I don't want "David" to hurt Casey or anyone else. My parents, sister, and I all sat at the table at my parents' house on Zoom and held hands when the judge said he was going to set the bail at $500,000. We were happy that it was a lot of money for him to be able to get out of jail for now.

MARY

The detective was able to find KK's attacker due to the video he had sent. He waited at his apartment until they saw him. He knew right away why they were there. He told the detective that the sex was consensual, but the detective said that the video made it clear that it was not.

He was not what I expected. He lives with his girlfriend of five years and has three young children. He is employed as a hair stylist in Reno. I think he just saw an opportunity and thought KK would not be able to cause him any trouble. Kailin, like many people with Down syndrome, does not often yell or scream and sometimes struggles with advocating for herself. She is very compliant, especially when she is confused or stressed, so she did not physically fight him. While that made her more vulnerable, I believe that it may also have kept her alive.

The arraignment and bail hearing were done via Zoom. All during the hearing, he cried and acted like he had no idea why he was there. Kailin, Eilish, and I all wrote victim statements that were read by the DA. Many newly arrested prisoners were at the group arraignment, and KK's case was the last one. It made me nervous that the judge worked with most of the (nonviolent) prisoners so that they could make bail and not be stuck in jail pending their trials due to Covid. When it was time for "David's" hearing, the DA described the crime and read our victim statements into the record. The judge was quiet throughout and then said that this crime was so heinous that he felt the only way to protect the community was to impose a $500,000 bail, with half cash required. We were very relieved and thankful.

EILISH

The weeks following the attack were long and draining. After about two weeks, my mom texted me that he had been caught and arrested. There aren't words for what that feeling was like. I was happy he had been caught, but scared to face the reality of who attacked and assaulted my sister. I don't know what I thought this person would be like, but he was certainly not it. He was in his thirties, was in a long-term relationship, had young children, and was a well-established hair stylist in Reno. He seemingly looked to have a "normal" life. I was shocked and scared. If someone so "normal" looking could do this, how could we ever feel safe again?

The night before the bail hearing I think I slept maybe an hour. The thought of this person being out in the public and able to take advantage of other people scared the hell out of me. The bail hearing was conducted over Zoom due to Covid-19. Seeing Kailin's reaction when he stood up in the holding area was devastating.

The reality of the situation all came crashing down and broke my heart even more than I thought was possible. Although I'm Kailin's younger sister, I have always felt this extreme responsibility to protect her. Knowing this person violated and took advantage of her, in this way especially, tore me to pieces.

The DA read the victim impact statements Kailin, my mom, and I wrote. It was confusing and frustrating seeing Kailin's assailant's reaction to everything. He was shaking his head in confusion and crying. How could he not understand why he was here and how much hurt he caused my sister and our family? At the end, the judge stated the only way to keep the public safe from such a "sick" person was to set his bail at $500,000. In Nevada, everyone is entitled to bail (unless it's a first-degree murder charge), so having the bail set so high was a bit of a relief for my family.

Recovery and Present Day

KAILIN

Now we are waiting to see if I have to testify at court. I hope he takes the plea deal so I don't have to go to court, but I will go to court if I have to. I want to protect people from getting hurt by him like I did. If I testify against "David," I will tell the whole world the full truth about what happened. I'm going to have to take him down in person.

I talked to a counselor for a while about my feelings on the phone. I was sad then, but now I'm not. My friends and family got me through it. To feel better, I wanted to find a new place that was right for me. I found a new home so I could be independent again and live on my own. I wasn't afraid to live on my own, and now it is my favorite home. I just know I like living on my own better. I'm really careful about locking my door, and I won't let anyone into my house unless it's my family or I know them. I'm more aware of my surroundings now. I think it's a good idea to live on your own when you go to college and get a job. I feel strong and brave now.

MARY

Due to Covid, preliminary hearings in Washoe County are very backed up. If there is a trial, it most likely will be over a year away. The mandatory sentence in Nevada for sexual assault is ten years to life, with ten years minimum before parole eligibility. Because KK is considered a vulnerable person, there is a consecutive eight to twenty years enhancement. The DA asked KK if she would agree to a plea bargain of dropping the enhancement if he pleads guilty to the sexual assault. Kailin and the rest of us liked that idea, so that she would not have to go through a trial. Now we are waiting to see if he accepts it. The DA feels like it is a good deal for "David," because he would most likely get a longer sentence if a jury saw the videos.

KK has been changed by this, as have all of us. I'm so glad we are a close-knit family and that she knew she could trust us to help guide her through this trauma. I am very thankful that she is alive and recovering. And very grateful that she has her sister to love and support her.

Kailin now questions her sexuality, wondering if she might be a lesbian. I support her right to explore her sexual orientation, although she never questioned her heterosexuality in the past. Because of this experience, which was an act of violence and not love, she thinks and says that a relationship with a man is not safe.

Kailin has proven to be very resilient. I don't know if she is just very strong or if her disability somehow affects her memory process or helps her to put things behind her. She is more reserved than before and keeps to herself more. She is currently doing music therapy and art therapy, which she enjoys. I think these alternate ways of expressing and dealing with her feelings will be more effective than just talk therapy.

Throughout this whole ordeal, I've been impressed and thankful for the professionalism and sensitivity of the police who responded, the detective who worked the case, the nurse and advocates at the Advocacy Center, the people from the district attorney's office (the assistant DA and the advocates), the judge in the case, and the staff at the Victims of Crime Program. I know the trauma could have been much worse for Kailin.

Kailin moved out again, into her own apartment, a few months after the attack. She loves her independence. I know that in a perfect world, Kailin and all people should be free of the fear of sexual violence. But this is not a perfect world and, unfortunately, bad people often seek out those who are trusting or vulnerable. Now that KK has experienced sexual violence, she is no longer naive and understands firsthand the importance of safety and security. I know that recovery will take time and that this has changed her forever. I am so very proud of Kailin's courage, strength, and resiliency.

EILISH

KK's assailant is still in custody as of early December 2020. I check the county jail website every day to make sure he's still there. We're currently waiting to see if he'll accept a plea deal or not. If not, we likely won't see a trial until late next year. It's been almost six months since the attack, and I still struggle on a daily basis with what happened. The guilt, sadness, and anger I feel is overwhelming at times. I'm so grateful my family is so close and so supportive of one another. The resiliency that Kailin and our entire family unit has shown during this is remarkable.

Since moving back out, I think KK has taken some of her power and control back. Her independence is what she prides herself on, so being able to move back out has been important for her. Covid has made it difficult for her to find work opportunities near her new apartment, but she's participating in several virtual art therapies and doing different activities with her service provider every week.

I text Kailin every single day to see what she's up to (and to make sure her door is locked). She's more reserved and keeps to herself more than she once did. I'm not sure where she's at with processing because she's not much of a talker. I often wonder if she's genuinely moving forward or if her disability makes it hard for her to put her feelings and experiences into words. I also worry that she will have difficulties with future romantic relationships because of this violent and traumatic experience.

I've realized that my parents, Kailin, and I will never be the same after this experience. I started referring to the period of time before this happened as the "sunshine and rainbows phase." This is the most difficult thing we've gone through as a family, but Kailin has led us with her resiliency, bravery, and strength. My mom has been such a rock during all of this as well! This experience has taught me a lot, but the most important thing it has taught me is how lucky I am to have such a strong big sister to look up to.

9

Spartan Kid

JOURNEYS

Brandon Baldwin

My name is Brandon Baldwin, and I am in my senior year of the Beyond Academics program at UNC Greensboro. I am excited about having the opportunity to share my journey with you. I've had some great and not-so-great experiences, but they have all taught me a lot. So here goes . . .

Let me tell you a little bit about myself. I have leukodystrophy, and as a result I struggle with apraxia of speech, dyslexia, recall, and processing disorders. This has made education and socializing very challenging for me. When I was in high school, I wanted to go to college like my brother and cousins had done. By the time I hit my junior year, I realized that might not happen. I had lots of amazing teachers, but two really influenced my life. Coach Fred Norris, who taught me history was always there for me and supported me in anything I wanted to do; he believed in me. Another teacher was Coach Ashton Peacock; she was my English teacher. She is the one who started my love for writing. Don't get me wrong, I hated English, but Coach Peacock encouraged me to write, and that is where I found myself. Because of all of that support, I knew I needed to try to figure out a way to go to college. My parents started looking into programs that might be a good fit for me. We lived in Texas, and there really weren't any good programs in the entire state. I know, hard to believe! So, we found a few on the East Coast and decided to visit them. We narrowed it down to three programs and visited those schools. The first two we visited were nice, but they were not for me. Then we visited UNC Greensboro and realized that was where I needed to be. My mom was worried about me being so far away from home, but we applied anyway. It was my senior year in high school, and we heard back from the Beyond Academics program that I was conditionally accepted, but I had to wait a year. The program at Beyond Academics was limited to a certain number of students, which is why I was wait-listed for a year. At first, we were sad because I wanted to go from high school to college, but now, looking back on it, it was the best choice for me. I used that year to get used to being out of my high school routine, and I learned how to do some of my chores on my own. I learned how to do my own laundry and keep my room and bathroom clean.

The next year, I started at UNC Greensboro. When I moved into the dorm, I had three roommates. I was nervous, but one of my roommates was in my program, and the other two were regular students and very nice. We all had our own room, and I shared a bathroom. I wanted to try everything at the college and join as much as I could. I was scared about being on my own, but I was ready to try it.

In my freshman year, I tried a lot of different clubs and sports. I started playing club tennis. I ended up playing club tennis for two years. We would play two to three times a week, and in my sophomore year we participated in a tournament in Wilmington, North Carolina, at UNC Wilmington. That was my first real college experience that took me out of my comfort zone. I rode to Wilmington with my teammates, and we stayed in a hotel. The first night that we got there, we went to a restaurant/bar that had a volleyball pit, and after we ate, we all played volleyball. Later that night, we went back to the hotel, where four of us stayed in and the rest of the group went out dancing. I had a lot of fun playing tennis, but unfortunately, I did not win. All in all, it was a great experience and a lot of fun. Of course, the trip did not end without incident. When we got back to campus, I gave money to the driver and my credit card fell out of my wallet. I went inside and realized it was missing, and I called my mom. She said to retrace my steps, and luckily, I found it on the sidewalk in front of my dorm.

Also, in my freshman year I was fortunate enough to meet Perry Flynn. Perry helped me get connected with Special Olympics and Unified Sports. Through Unified Sports I helped and participated in basketball and football. I participated in Unified Sports my sophomore and junior years, and going into my senior year Perry offered me the position as club leader for Unified Sports. As the club leader, some of my responsibilities are getting the participants stretched out, advertising for Unified Sports, and making everyone feel like they are part of the group and valued. Another awesome opportunity that Perry gave me was to be the honorary team captain for the division three soccer championship that was being held at UNC Greensboro. I had the opportunity to go on the field, holding a soccer ball as they announced my name and fist-pumping with all of the players. Perry also hooked me up with two opportunities for internships. One of them was helping with horses and the other was helping out at a local coffee shop. He has definitely been a great support and mentor for me.

I've had a lot of great teachers during my four years, but a couple of them really become very important to me. In my freshman year, I met one of my teachers, Jessica Besaw. I instantly felt a bond with her. Shortly thereafter, I met Dr. Lalenja Harrington, who I call Dr. La. Both of these wonderful professors have been very influential in my life. They have both been there for me and encouraged me to follow my dreams. In the fall of my sophomore year, Jessica sent an email to everyone about the first TEDx Talks being held at UNC Greensboro. My first reaction was to close the email and I said no, but then I felt a strong urging from God that I needed to pursue it. I emailed Jessica that night and asked her if we could meet the next day. We met that day, and Jessica said that she didn't think anyone would take the opportunity, but she was glad that I did. Jessica gave me her cell phone number and said if I have any questions, I could call her anytime. I went to the café and sat down, and I started writing my submission. When I finished, I emailed my submission in, and the next week they contacted me and said I had been selected to participate in TEDx. Over the next few months, I worked with Dr. La and Jessica on my speech and presentation. In the spring of my sophomore year, I participated in TEDx and won the night! Here is a link to the talk if you're interested in seeing my presentation. After I did TEDx, Dr. La told me about an opportunity to speak at the annual ARC Convention for the state of Virginia. It was held at James Madison University, and I gave my talk there. Of course, my presentation wasn't without incident because I fell off of the stage. In an effort to try and save another speaker as they were falling off the back of the stage, I went down as well! Overall it was an awesome experience, one that I will never forget!

In my sophomore year, I participated in a research project conducted by Lindsey Oaks. They asked me to be in a photograph with her that is on the UNC Greensboro website about her research project. I also applied for a scholarship in my sophomore year that I was awarded for the fall semester of my junior year.

In my junior year, I moved into an apartment with two of my friends that are in the Beyond Academics program. One of my roommates is my best friend Demarcus Mobley. He and I have been roommates since our freshman year, and we have done a lot of fun things together. I got an internship at Downtown Hownds working in a doggy day care.

My boss, Holly Anderson, is great to work for, and she has taught me a lot. My other big accomplishment in my junior year is I started a club for the Beyond Academics students called Beyond Awesome. I wanted the Beyond Academics students to have a place where we could get to know each other better and make friends. I planned a lot of fun activities; some of them were movie night, a scavenger hunt around campus, attending a basketball game together, board game night, and dodgeball.

I have also had a few crazy experiences over the past three

years. The first and maybe one of the most memorable ones was the "counterfeit incident." I was sitting down in the café having lunch, and this guy approached me and asked me if I had change for a twenty-dollar bill. I gave him two tens and he gave me a twenty. He left and five minutes later I saw him walking back in my direction with a police officer. I looked down at the twenty-dollar bill and I realized it was counterfeit. I went to the Beyond Academics office and told my support what had happened, and he went with me to the campus police office. We told the police officer what had happened, and he said yes that they had several calls about this man. He took me into the back to identify the man through a plexiglass window. I said that I wasn't sure which one he was because I was afraid he could see me and then he would come after me. We then sat in an interrogation room for forty minutes waiting. After twenty minutes, my support needed to leave, and he said, "You'll be fine," and he left. The police officer asked me some questions, and then I was on my way; of course, I never did get my twenty dollars back.

And the last, but not least, of my crazy experiences involves riding public transportation. During group support, we practice a lot of different skills, one being riding public transportation. The first time I rode public transportation, a man asked me for money and scared the Scooby Doobie snacks out of me! The next time that I was supposed to ride the bus with my support group, I told my support that I didn't like to ride the bus because every time I did something bad happened. There were four of us, and we all got on the bus and headed downtown toward the depot. When it was time to get off the bus, usually I check to see if my wallet is in my pocket, but this time for some reason I didn't. After we got off the bus and started walking, I checked my pocket, and my phone was there but my wallet was gone. I was very sad, and I went running back to the bus to try to find my wallet. There were two people on the bus that said that they didn't see my wallet and that they had just gotten on, so after looking on the bus I got off and I called my mom and said that I guess I need to cancel my card because I've lost my wallet again. We went to the authorities at the depot and filed a report, and then we all sat on chairs, and as a group we decided we would go home in an Uber since I didn't have my Spartan card to be able to get back home on the bus. I was going to use my phone to call an Uber, but my phone was dead, so my support was going to use his phone to go on Uber, and his phone was dead.

The other three guys in the group didn't have an Uber account on their phones. Luckily, my Beyond Academics support had brought a charger with him, and he charged his phone so that he could make the call. It was raining and freezing cold, and of course, the bright-eyed student that I am, I only had on shorts and a T-shirt, and I was freezing. We took an Uber home, and I'd like to say the story ended there, but it didn't. My mom said that the student card center was still open, and I should take twenty dollars and go get a new Spartan card. I ran like a flash in the freezing cold rain to the card center, got my new card, and, voilà, my tragic day had ended! And now you know why I don't like, nor will I ride, buses!

So now that brings me to my senior year and my plans for my future. My first love is writing and creating. I write poemsongs, which are poems with a meaning, set to music. I also write poems stories. My dream job would be to write meaningful poemsongs and stories that motivate and encourage people. I have developed a website where I post all of my work. Hopefully someday I will be able to make a living from my writing, but in the meantime, I really like working with other people with disabilities. Since I like sports so much, I would love to work with kids with disabilities in a sports setting.

In conclusion, I wouldn't change anything in the past four years. I have had a great experience at UNC Greensboro, and I have learned a lot. I will miss college, but I am ready and excited to start the next chapter of my life. I wanted to end my chapter with a couple of my poemsongs. If you're interested in reading more of my work, my website is https://www.beaconhillpoet.com.

Heroize Job Edition

They told ME You are a
Disgrace for the country
you think our Company wants a
Disability waste
like YOU
I said just Try me listen to this
I have plenty of skill in me if
you just trust me
but they shunned me away
that's why I'm writing this today
Ay
God I Pray my music travels to the right ears so they can hear the Heartaches we take to find a decent job that not only pays the bills but also makes this life fun that's all we want like anyone else not to be discriminized just an Option in life to be
Heroized

Do we look like a Disgrace?

I don't think so
we are just people
with these Strengths
you call Disability
I call adversity
cuz you're scaredly
holding your ears
barely
to know the truth
the Reality
we are
no
hallucinations
we are
spit balling
hints
I guess

you don't get it
we are for real
how many times
do I need to drill that in your head
to hear
we're always one step ahead

I'm
B.H
you're right
I'm weak I don't know how to speak
no one reads my pipe dream
they say Constantly
how about you go sell your soul at a Dead end job cuz you're flippin and a floppin hoping to strike it big never gonna pick up a mic
kid
this music thing is too hard
get rid of your thoughts
you got no shot

you're a Disability
with no idea
how to start
just stop
and breathe
and see
it doesn't matter how well you are Dressed you will always be Undressed as a Disability
Checked by Security
your Poetry is nothing
this is Reality
Listen
real Closely
Kid
you don't see
you're

Running
And you're
Trying

And you're prying
Every shy moment
Into lyrics
thinking you can be the next Revolutionary
Disability
Movement
With Apraxia
and Dyslexia
HAHA
I said
Watch me

Black Eye (R) Word

Don't Rush Greatness

Greatness doesn't come in one day
Greatness is in the work you play
in my gym
(The Lord's Gym)
and then
he Explained
don't waste time
worrying about the person
you won't be
you will be
the person I sent you down to be to make them free
Write a Dream
and see a podium under your feet
but you gotta wait and see sometimes you just gotta breathe
(and breathe)
It's not what you show
(the finished product)

No
It's the breeze to the project
how you process
greatness is what you don't show!!!
Greatness is how many times you get knocked down stressed out but you know (You Know)
your Story must be told
even if people see you as a ghost an (R) Word Disability (F) Word
but you believe God is upward seeing your pain won't go
unnamed
you're a name
that is already
unblamingly Great
you're not a fake like those bullies who try to take what makes you great Greatness is not what you take
Greatness is the many days You grind and grinded
Through the bad times
Thinking you'll never be knighted Where you wanted
All those years you fought
thought it was for nothing
But that's the greatness
About you
You never stop Tryin
You're brave like a Lion
you might be a breed of a Disability but you're a poet
Speak to them,
Let them see
what you're thinking
I say, never ever Dying
but Reality
I am, Always Forever Dying inside
cuz on one side
the Bullies what they say really feel like they're driving what Confidence I gain in my own grave
when I die
but God I don't wanna die

so
everyday
I'm Praying to you Lord on my knees to help me to
Gain the Words What I believe what I gotta say
There's always a day
for the bad to go away
and the crap you're Pushing through
will
Fly
like how a butterfly fly away,
and that's the day
When people see A Flightless bird Like me
Celebrate we
have wings
Beautiful ones
you didn't see
I just wanna be me
but you hit me with the right That symbolize

a black eye
every time
you say
the (R) Word in front of me I wanna scream but I Express my anger in my writing
no one sees

cuz I'm a so called
Disability

when I put my Game face on They laugh and Leave But My Story must be told I cannot Fold
You can't Hold
This Disability boy
down
My Greatness is Gonna be told

10

Best Experiences at IDEAL

De'Onte Brown, Deriq Graves, Nadia Osbey, Breyan Pettaway, and Sayid Webb

Editor's Note: The following is from students at Georgia State University discussing their experiences in IDEAL (Inclusive Digital Expression and Literacy).

My name is Sayid Webb, I am twenty-two years old and a second-year student at the IDEAL program. My experience during college is just like I dreamed it to be. I go to Georgia State University, and I am enrolled in the GSU IDEAL program. In my first year, I was a little bit nervous until I saw my old friends from Warren Tech. Warren Technical School is a trade school in DeKalb County, Georgia, for students aging from sixteen to twenty-two where we learned about different job industries and received training according to interest. Through the many programs, I was able to gain experience in graphic design, and that's where I was recommended to apply for the IDEAL program at Georgia State. In IDEAL, I used my graphic design skills for events, invitations, and parties. For example, to plan for our past Halloween party in 2019, I was able to make the flyer, poster, and tickets to promote the event. We began the planning process in September to make sure that we had everything in order. My favorite memory is the annual Halloween party, and I became the host and designed all the invitations. We had a great time at the Halloween party. IDEAL helped me to intern at EXLAB at Georgia State University. I was a student assistant where I was able to be at the front desk, attend training and workshops, and shadow other students while they were working. My favorite part of the internship was giving the students a tour of the EXLAB because I was able to use the skills I learned while giving tours at the APEX Museum. I like to volunteer at the football and basketball games with Nadia and Deonte, my friends I have met at IDEAL. In the future, I look forward to creating my own graphic design and photography business. I was even thinking about doing something in the music industry. With the graphic design, I plan to host events such as birthday parties or just any type of celebration.

My name is Breyan Pettaway, and I am twenty-two years old. I have been a part of the IDEAL program for a year now. I love to write short stories, play video games like *Fallout 4* and *Sims,* and watch YouTube. I am going to graduate next year. IDEAL has helped me with some of my social problems, and I have enjoyed my time here and the relationships I've made with people in IDEAL. The stories that I write are fan fiction writing, usually anime crossovers or similar to these, and I usually post the stories on Wattpad, where my username is Firebreather238. My favorite anime I watch are *My Hero Academia, High School DxD, Highschool of the Dead, Naruto* (not *Boruto*), *The Seven Deadly Sins, Demon King Daimao,* and *Heaven's Lost Property.* My time with IDEAL was always a place to relax when I was somewhat stressed out. My closest friend within IDEAL is Deriq, and we talk about story ideas and what outcomes would be cool for each story. I have made some connections to some of the peer mentors, and they have provided help in some of my classes and in my story writing. I'm not sure what I plan to do after college, but I am open to what is to come.

My name is De'Onte Brown. I am twenty-four years old, and I like to play video games and meet new people. I've graduated from Georgia State, and I have enjoyed meeting new people and just being a part of the college campus—going to classes and having fun on campus. I will say the peer mentors play a big part in our lives or roles because without them we wouldn't be where we are today, and it's thanks to them that we got this far in the first place. Thank you, peer mentors, for your support and guidance and leadership. I work at O'Neill Communications, and I got a chance to edit videos and make my own videos on YouTube. There were some struggles to make these videos, but I overcame and persevered. I got a chance to take what I learned from video editing and tied it into my final project, a mini video series called *Shaking It Up with De'Onte.* I know it came out great! I also got a chance to work at CNN and edit videos for the news and the media source. I also got a chance to make my own video there as well for a project that I was doing. Though my time there got cut short due to Covid-19, it was very fun and I got to work beside two very special people as well, Ben and Sophia. It was fun working with Sophia because once I got used to the schedule I would have certain days where I would come alone, and I would work with Sophia throughout the whole entire day. I thought that was very cool that I was taking a big step on working by myself without my job coach/peer mentor Ben. I also got a chance to work with my best friend and my peer mentor Ben, which was very fun. Simon was very cool too. I just hope to have more opportunities like this in the future.

My name is Deriq Graves, and I am in my second year of college. I am twenty-two years old. My goal is to be a great actor and a story-writer. One thing I like about the IDEAL program is the costume party; that was a lot of fun hanging out with good friends, dressing up in costumes, and playing games like UNO. IDEAL has helped me by making great friends and having people by my side who care about me and support me in my goal to become an actor and storywriter. My time at college has been great, thanks to them. Some of my work includes *Fantasy Land,* a story I am working on for school, where a man goes on an adventurer to kill the Goblin King and becomes the world's greatest hero. The story has our hero, Bill Garter, and a small group of friends go to the home of the Goblin King and kill him, but there is a twist near the end of the story . . . but you'll have to read it to find out! The reason I did this story is that I like making action stories where you don't know how it is going to end. One of the ways IDEAL has helped me is by finding programs with story writing for me to join, like dramatic writing and short screenwriting.

My name is Nadia Osbey. I am twenty-three and I've been with IDEAL from 2019 to 2020. I enjoy hanging out with my friends and going to CMII. The CMII stands for Creative Media Industries Institute, and it is located on Georgia State's campus. There people can go to hang out, take creative media classes, and attend workshops. My friends and I would always go there to eat lunch and play with the VR goggles. My favorite part of IDEAL was getting an internship at the Panthers' football stadium and working with people who love sports, just like me. At the stadium, I was in charge of data entry for marketing (that's where I learned to use Excel) and working the football/basketball games. At the games, I was in charge of directing people to their seats. I was also a part of our Special Olympics basketball team! I've learned a lot and grown a lot through this program, and I'm thankful for the opportunities that the people of IDEAL have given me to go to college.

11

Two Poems

Carly O'Connell

Poem #1 Up to the Sky

I took my red pen
to write my name
but nothing appeared
on the paper.
Up in the sky
each letter etched.
Why doesn't it come down? I want to please
touch the sky.

Poem #2

How would you like it if you only could eat people?
I can only eat nothing.
People are like how it feels to be called sorry.

12

Goal(s) in Common

Hannah Lenae Humes

I was born in 2001 and that same year
the first girl with Down syndrome
graduated from a local high school
with an academic diploma.
What did this mean? Could I, someday,
also graduate from high school?
Goal in common.
I went to a typical preschool so I
could model my friends and practice
language. We played together, sat in
circle time together, ate snacks together.
Goals in common.
I had access to the general education
curriculum all through elementary
school.
I modeled my peers; I learned to follow
the routine; I learned to keep my hands
to myself; I learned to follow directions;
I was accountable for my
behavior; I made friends; I learned to
read and write (at my level).
Goals in common.
I transitioned to middle and high school.

I had access to the general education
curriculum. I modeled my peers; I
worked within groups; I
learned about responsibility; I
participated in clubs; I went to
Homecoming; I went to sports events; I
made friends; I volunteered in our
community center for work experience;
I toured college campuses.
Goals in common.
Senior year I filled out college
applications; I was interviewed by
college programs; I celebrated college
acceptance with friends.
Goals in common.
Then . . . Covid-19 happened in the
spring of 2020. I finished my senior
year in remote learning.
I graduated high school just like the girl did
in 2001, but my graduation was virtual.
I started my college career as a
Freshman participating in remote
classes.
NOT A GOAL IN COMMON but a
reality in common.
I haven't been able to meet anyone in
person yet, only via Zoom, but I can't
wait.
I haven't been able to take a class on
campus yet, only via Zoom, but I can't
wait.
I haven't been able to participate in
clubs or sports yet on campus, only via
Zoom, but I can't wait.

Being tutored via Zoom has been hard
for me.
Learning cooking skills via a computer
has been hard for me.
Sometimes I get headaches.
Alongside my Next Steps classes and
electives, I'm learning about time
management, computer skills, how to be a
better communicator and how to cope
with so many Zoom meetings. I
exercise and keep an exercise log. I'm
doing my best at journaling and
completing homework. It's good to
keep busy! I love my Vanderbilt class
called American Popular
Music! I am motivated to learn by
my love of music. I have a learning
agreement with my professor. Instead of
tests I do projects like making a music
history timeline and creating a digital
poster of Taylor Swift.
I think my instructors and ambassadors
are so smart and friendly; they are the
best. Anchor Down!
I am happy that I don't have to wear a
mask all day! I want Covid-19 to go
away!
Goal(s) in common.

13

I Did What They Said I Couldn't

Allen Thomas

My name is Allen Thomas. I am a graduate of Appalachian State University's Scholars with Diverse Abilities Program (SDAP). I am a student currently at the University of North Carolina Leadership Education in Neurodevelopmental Disorders program, which is a one-year program where I work with doctors, physical therapists, and occupational therapists, and we discuss topics around disability laws, and I also will begin Wake Tech Community College in January. My major is early childhood education, because I want to help families with early intervention resources. Coming to Appalachian State was a really new experience for me. It was the first time I was ever away from home. I learned to self-advocate by asking my professors about different assignments. App State set a tone that anybody can be successful no matter where they came from. Different from high school, all the staff at App State wanted to talk about my future and taught me about being a successful student. Prior to App State, I've never done anything on my own or socialized. Freshman orientation at App State helped me a lot by making new friends and doing things for myself. I also made friends all over campus, and I was respected by my professors. In high school, I used to stay in my room all day playing video games because I didn't have a social support system. Socially at App State, I would go to church with friends, go out to dinner, and go to Washington, D.C.

Up until App State, all of my former teachers, with the exception of a few, said I had no future and my job choices would be picking up trash and working in retail. I was in the occupational courses of study program where you learn and find job placement, but they said I would never go to college. Here I am, years later, accepted into my third university. Without a program like SDAP we would be stuck with no social life or career path.

14

Climbing Higher and "From Mission Impossible to Mission Possible"

Courtney Jorgensen

Introduction: Hi, I'm Courtney Jorgensen. This submission is about a project I did as part of my inclusive higher education program (Aggies Elevated at Utah State University, USU) and how that project represents some amazing aspects of the program.

Each year USU invites the different school clubs and organizations to create a design that represents their group and then paint it on a section of the road on campus. Last year (2019) our Aggies Elevated instructors told us about this and showed us a picture of the design they had done the year before. I decided I wanted to try and create the design for our Aggies Elevated group that year. I chose the Aggies Elevated logo as my inspiration. This was my final design.

Looking at my design, you can see there are a lot of things about it that represent the Aggies Elevated experience. For instance:

The color: Blue is one of the school colors of USU, which is the home of the Aggies Elevated program. The different shades of blue are like the different people in the program. We each have our own unique strengths and challenges.

The mountains: The increasing heights of the mountains represent the obstacles we face in life. As we overcome small challenges, we develop the strength, skills, and confidence to tackle and overcome greater challenges.

Figure 14.1.
The author's Aggies Elevated design

The initials: In this design the "E" appears to be supporting the "A." In Aggies Elevated, the amazing staff and mentors teach and support us. The students also help one another in different ways. The "A" at the top of the highest summit could represent reaching our potential.

The Aggies Elevated program truly is about helping each other and learning to "Climb Higher."

One of the ways the Aggies Elevated staff helped me was to suggest I consider submitting a presentation for the State of the Art Student Leadership Conference this year (2020). The topic I chose for that was about overcoming obstacles to attending an inclusive higher education program, like Aggies Elevated, and how to prepare for that. That way other students could have the same amazing kind of opportunity I have had. That presentation is titled "From Mission Impossible to Mission Possible."

"From Mission Impossible to Mission Possible"

Hi, I'm Courtney Jorgensen. I chose to do this presentation about overcoming obstacles to attending an inclusive higher education program like the one I attended (Aggies Elevated at USU) and how to prepare for that, so that other students could have the same amazing kind of opportunity I have had. You can view the video or read the transcript in the digital edition of this book.

15

Inclusive College on Zoom?

MY INCLUSIVE HIGHER EDUCATION 2020 EXPERIENCE

Stephen Wanser, Kate Lisotta, and Kim Dean

This chapter is about me and how I'm doing with the transition of being online in an inclusive college program. I worked with a peer mentor and a professor to reflect on my experiences and write up my thoughts and insights. We did it all through Zoom in less than four weeks.

Please enjoy what I am about to share.

My name is Stephen Stone Wanser. I am twenty-two years old when writing this in 2020. I am from Philadelphia, Pennsylvania, and I attend the Raising Expectations for Academic Learning (REAL) Certificate at Arcadia University in Glenside, Pennsylvania. I have the heart of a lion, but I fight like a bull. Some characteristics that describe me would be: I am funny, smart, and talented. My hobbies are made from my characteristics, and these hobbies include playing video games, writing, and cooking.

I also like to describe myself as smart because I am motivated about school. I motivate myself because I want to make good grades and make everyone in my life proud. I am also an overachiever, and I seem to find myself going above and beyond for assignments and projects as well. I also have trained myself to follow directions. I learned that if you look deep into directions, you will always find it easier to complete tasks.

I finished high school in 2020, and now I'm attending Arcadia University. Arcadia is a small, beautiful campus with a very noticeable big castle. The location is in Montgomery County, in Cheltenham Township, near Philadelphia. In general, Arcadia has small class sizes, so it is easy to get to know each other and professors.

I am in the REAL Certificate. This is from the website (https://www.arcadia.edu/majors-and-programs/real-certificate/): "The REAL Certificate allows students with disabilities to experience college through academic, vocational, and social programs. Within 2 years, students will take a minimum of one undergraduate course per semester, receive tutoring, social support, and job shadowing. This program is approved by the U.S. Department of Education so students can apply for federal aid."

Our Collaboration Method

We started meeting in September and met twice a week. I am surprised that we did all this in four weeks. We started with a brainstorm, we thought about who would read this, we thought about tips. Here is a link to our original brainstorm document with all the ideas and work we added. Toward the end, we read it together and agreed on the work. The last thing we did was write questions and record a Zoom interview, which you can see in the digital edition of this book.

My Experiences in the REAL Certificate Program (Inclusive Higher Education)

When I found out that I was going to college, I was looking forward to getting a better education and making new friends. But then came the virus, not a computer virus!! So I was starting Arcadia during a pandemic!

When I found out we were going to be remote for school, I was sad and happy. Sad because I was really looking forward to being on campus. But at the same time I'm happy because I get to stay home and learn, and I find it easier to do school work while being home. Since the pandemic started, learning through (Arcadia) Zoom University has allowed me to learn in the comfort of my own home without distractions. At home I don't have to worry about a lot of noise. Typically, this program is in person, but since there is a pandemic my experience has been online. I go to Pajama University.

The best part of college so far is meeting different people and learning the ways they think and what their thoughts are about things. I enjoy learning from other pieces of peoples' ideas and twisting them into a new idea. Finally, peer mentors are the best thing that you're ever gonna have! Having a peer mentor comes in handy. They can help you come up with ideas and guide you in the right direction for assignments. You are able to come up with ideas, but they help to keep them organized and edit them, which is useful.

Another good part of the REAL program is social time. This happens every day, and it depends on your class schedule what time you have it. Social time is the best time ever to get to watch YouTube videos or relax with other peers.

A few things were hard for me when we started online college. For example, how the heck to work Zoom?! And all the many different Zoom links! It was challenging that there were too many changes in the Zooms when we started. Another bummer about being remote was I didn't get to see or really meet new people in person.

But the good news is there are lots of chances to make new friends in remote settings. Here are a few examples. Example one: giving phone numbers out. One time I had to exchange phone numbers with one of my social peer mentors to stay in contact. It worked out very well. It felt weird at first to give out my phone number, but now I am used to it. When my usual friends are busy, it's nice to have other people to talk to. I'm both an introvert and an extrovert. I definitely like to be alone sometimes to have time to think. I also definitely do like to socialize once I get to know the group and the people. It doesn't take me long to figure out who I want to spend time with. If you pay attention to people, you can figure out which ones are good friend material. Example two: I get put into breakout rooms with random people I don't know at first. At orientation we were placed into breakout rooms. I was put into a breakout room with a person I had never met before. I was worried he didn't want to talk to me because his camera kept turning off. However, it turned out we were both into anime and it was fun to talk to each other.

Online College: Challenges and Tips

As I said, managing all the Zoom was difficult. Recently, I thought I had English class and I logged on, but then I realized we didn't have class. The teacher emailed me to let me know that we are only working on a discussion board for this week. It was kind of confusing because he was not entirely clear about when we were meeting. Usually, I'm very organized, but it's easy to get confused with your schedule for online school. Always check your syllabus or assignments and pay attention during class to keep track of class dates. If you are ever confused, you can reach out to your professor.

ADVICE AND TIPS FOR STUDENTS

- Organization and Planning: Be Prepared
  - Stay organized with the Zoom links for classes. Use one document with course links instead of scrolling through old emails or Canvas pages.
  - Keep your schedule up on your phone. Look at it every morning to know what to do and keep track of when classes are happening.
  - Make sure that you get enough sleep to be able to focus in class.
  - Make sure you eat breakfast so you are not hungry during classes.

  - Look at your email every day to make sure you know what is happening.
- Participation in Online Learning
  - Pay attention.
    - Keep phone on silent. Turn off email notifications.
    - Plan for your pets ahead of time.
    - Take notes. You never know! Then look at your notes throughout the week.
    - Make sure you look frozen. Look at the screen and stay still. If you don't stay pretty still, it is going to look like you are not paying attention.
    - Plan focus. Reduce other tabs on your computer.
  - Keep your camera on or, if not, make sure you try to say something during the Zoom or at least say something in the chat so they know you are there.
  - Try to stay on your camera so your professor knows you are there and paying attention.
  - If you look at the computer screen for a really long time and it is bothering you, try to look away from the screen at a wall to blink and refresh.
  - Depending on your teacher, you may be able to take quick breaks or turn off your camera briefly while still listening to the class.
- Social Tips
  - Our program only lasts for two years. Enjoy it while you can! :)
  - Try to be yourself.
  - If you don't know other people and are shy, you can sit back in the beginning to get a feel for the group. As you become more comfortable, you can start to speak up to try to make friends.
  - You can use the chat feature if you don't want to speak out loud or have any technical issues.
  - It can be easier to make friends if you are paying attention and listening to the professor. If you don't, you may end up messing up and not being a good team member.

- o You can pay attention to the way people in the class work and think, which can help you figure out who is friend material.

COVERSATION: CONVERSATION WHILE COVERED UP

We will be back on campus some day! How can we get along with social distancing next year when REAL is on campus again? We will end our chapter with ideas about "Coversation!" We offer tips for inclusive higher education in the new mask-wearing world. Mask wearing while having conversation = Coversation!

It is harder to hear and follow a conversation when you are both wearing masks, and we tried to think about good tips for college life with masks. Our first idea was to use future technology!! Maybe we will invent a Google Translate mask that will show your comments on your mask while you talk. But until we get there, we had a few ideas:

- When friends or teachers can't hear you, text your comment! Use your phone to dictate by tapping the microphone and hitting the text button.
- Make sure to look at people.
- Smile even when your mouth isn't showing. Your eyes look friendly!
- Use your hands a little more (thumbs-up, for example).
- Be considerate and keep your mask on inside.
- Professors should write stuff up on the board or on the screen as a backup.

I can't wait until I am back on campus and can have in-person "coversations!" By the time we come out of quarantine, Mask-ylvania (Pennsylvania) will be full of Philly cheesesteaks, Eagles fans, and history buffs. Hopefully you'll come to the City of Brotherly Love. Good things happen in Philadelphia!

If you feel comfortable and want to go for it, definitely do online learning if that is right for you! (Even if it's not at Arcadia.)

16

Inclusive College for All and How My Perception of My History Prof Changed

Keiron Dyck

Inclusive College for All

My name is Keiron. In May 2020, I completed the requirements for the Scholars with Diverse Abilities Program (SDAP) at Appalachian State University (App State). Since completing the program, I have been working with a support person at my local Vocational Rehabilitation office. I have been to a few job interviews at grocery stores, but my work opportunities are limited now because of the global pandemic. In the future, my goal is to work in the field of public history.

When I was a young child, I was diagnosed with disabilities. I have overcome them through dedication and hard work, and I was able to go to college through SDAP. SDAP is an Inclusive Postsecondary Education Program (IPSE) at App State. IPSEs, according to the Project 10 website are "programs that provide access to people with intellectual disabilities to postsecondary education." SDAP is a two-year non-degree-seeking program for people who have moderate to mild intellectual disabilities.

I like SDAP because some of the classes I got to take out of self-interest—for example, my history and drama classes. I have always been fascinated with American history and got to take this class in my final semester. My public history class was the most impactful because it showed me how history could be experienced outside of an academic setting. I liked this class because I am hoping to have a job in this field. This class, and the other history classes I took, helped me think about jobs that could connect people with history. Maybe I could work as a guide or a docent at a museum or historical site. I am sure that I will continue to read and write and think about historical events. I also took drama classes. These classes focused on acting, which has always been interesting to me. I really enjoyed being on a stage and performing scenes with people. I am interested in being a museum tour guide or a tour guide on a Civil War battlefield or in making a podcast drama about certain historical events.

I enjoyed having a campus job, which was part of my SDAP experience. My favorite job was working at one of the movie theaters as part of the film staff. I liked having a job because it was part of my independence, and also I liked filling a role that needed to be filled. The main reason why I like SDAP and why I think every college should have an IPSE is because these meaningfully build independence. When I began SDAP, I had had limited opportunities to make my own choices. As a student in SDAP, I had to live on my own, make my own choices about meals, and set my own schedule and routine. SDAP expected me to show up on time for my job, classes, and other functions. For some of the classes, I had in-class support. I generally had a strong grasp of the material, but because they attended the class with me, I could use them as resources. They helped me take notes, and we would have conversations about class topics. One of these supports is now my best friend, Maggie.

I think every college institution should have an IPSE because it benefits the typical learners and the atypical learners. My friend, Maggie, explained that for the typical learners it's helpful to have an atypical learner as a student or friend because that way the typical learner can learn more about disabilities through actually seeing it, rather than reading about it. It makes it more real to be able to see it firsthand. For atypical learners who want to go to college, they have a natural curiosity to continue their learning to the next level, and they should be able to fulfill that curiosity. Programs like SDAP can't scale easily because they're designed to be a small, tight-knit unit, and they should remain small and be everywhere. It only makes sense for there to be more programs like SDAP.

How My Perception of My History Prof Changed

When I first saw Dr. Michaels, I knew this class was going to be trouble. I'd been waiting to take an American history class for as long as I'd been in college. I was finally going to engage with my favorite subject! But the prof looked stern and unapproachable. Then I turned around and met my in-class support person. "Support" looked bored as he scrolled through his phone. He didn't even look at me as he gave a thumbs-up. I was feeling more concerned.

Dr. Michaels went through his course syllabus and explained the expectations for the six required papers. Bottom line: he wouldn't accept late assignments for any reason. As I left the room, I felt super anxious about the class. I turned to ask "Support" for some help. He said, "Facts! Cool!" and then walked away. I was afraid I had made a mistake.

However, the material still interested me. I read the textbook and wrote my first paper. I was optimistic and I put a lot of work into it. I handed my paper in on time. I got an F.

"Support" was nowhere to be found. I was feeling desperate and super sure that I was going to fail the class. I pushed down my dread. I sent Dr. Michaels a note and we made an appointment to meet.

When I first met with Dr. Michaels, I understood that this would be a tough class for me, but it would be a good class. Dr. Michaels explained what he was looking for in that first F paper and in the papers that I still needed to write. He agreed that I could write three papers instead of six papers. Dr. Michaels gave me confidence that I could succeed in this class. When I expressed the concern that I felt I talked too much in his class, he said, "No! Do more of that!" He went on to say that he wished all his students asked questions and were interested in the material the same way I was. Later I found out that Dr. Michaels forgot that I was in SDAP because of how impressed he was with me as a student. He was saying to me that I was like everyone else in that class.

At the end of the semester, Dr. Michaels told me that I had gotten an A in the course. He said that if I had been taking the class for credit, I would have gotten a high grade as well.

My initial perception of the class was totally wrong. This was one of the most satisfying classes I was in at App State. "Support" not needed.

17

Qua's GT Excel Life and "Never Give Up"

Marquavious Barnes

My first year of college went well; I was just getting to know Georgia Tech and trying to navigate places to go and where to find friends. I had to focus on making good grades. I did good in all my classes, but as time went on my career grades didn't look too good, but I was glad when I had my past internships. I used to see my friends there. I liked it better when I was working for sports. Now, I will be working for the BuzzCard office. I like being up and walking around but not always. I need to sit down at least one time at work. My legs are like noodles, but my upper body is strong. I could go work out at a gym called the Campus Recreation Center.

I don't know if it was my first year or second, I refereed flag football and did some scorekeeping for volleyball. In flag football, I remembered I just let the boys play. I didn't throw any flags. I reffed frat teams. I wasn't that good at refereeing. I wanted to be the referee GOAT (Greatest of All Time). In volleyball, on the other hand, I was keeping up with the game. Volleyball is a fast-paced sport, so I had to focus. I'd get mad when I would mess up. I also worked for Barnes & Noble. I didn't really like working for B&N because I didn't like standing in one place all day. I'm the type of person that likes moving around.

My third year of college went well, but I didn't care about my grades or anything that year. I was mostly worried about surviving that year. I kind of was angry over something that happened in

2019 in the springtime in my social life. So, I was defending myself at all costs. People knew what the deal was if they said something to me. People knew I was still upset because I'd go places frowning. If you wanted to play around with me, I was not tolerating it. All I liked doing was being with friends or being alone playing my video games. I feel like playing video games helps you get your anger out.

My third year, in 2020, I remember I made a rap called "Never Give Up." I shocked everybody with my rap, and I have a tattoo that says "never give up." The meaning behind that rap was I want to change Excel for the better or worse. Then, in March of 2020, Covid-19 hit and messed everything up. We were out for five months. I'm glad I could take a break, because I was about to lose it in school because of something that happened in February of 2020. A girl got upset with me and caused some problems that were stressful. Now, it's my fourth year and I don't have a roommate. Donald Anderson was supposed to be my roommate, but it changed. I like living alone to have more space and be able to manage my own time without worrying about anyone else. I'm living in the moment every day; I'm a senior. I'm not worried about these girls, but I opened up for only two, and I said if they want to live in the moment with me, they can. I want a relationship and am trying to find the right person. This year, I'm more laid back and calm. I got good grades in all my classes, but I want to end my college year with all As. After college, I plan on moving back home to Athens, Georgia, and working there in the downtown area at a hotel or at the University of Georgia.

"Never Give Up"

Verse

The teachers tried me the students try me I never give up said I
never give up the students try me the teachers look right by me
Yeah, I will never give up

Chorus

I never give up said I never give up when life seems hard, I will never give up I never give up said I never give up I got it tatted I never give up

Verse

Never give up you don't know my circumstance yep, I will never give up one more year that I'm sentenced here 2021 I'm gone

Chorus

I never give up said I never give up when life seems hard, I never give up I never give up said I never give up I got it tatted I never give up

18

Photo Essays and Selections from Student Leadership Conference 2019

Breana Whittlesey, Kaelan Knowles, Elise McDaniel, Kenneth Kelty, Katie Bartlett, and Rachel Mast

Rachel Mast

College to me means:

College means to me to focus on college and to be on top of things. I need to work on skills and independent living. Do your homework and always show people around on campus. Can stay in dorms. It is cool to be at college.

What is your favorite class in college? And why?

My favorite classes are acting, hospitality class, and my academic class. We do a lot of cool work in acting and do hospitality job skills.

One rough thing that happened in college was:

It was rough for me because I have roommates [who] did not include me to do things with them. It was rough and hard, and I was upset that beginning year. I felt abandoned from my roommates last year, and they let me do nothing with them.

Elise McDaniel

What College Means to Me:

College to me means that I can be independent in different ways. My name is Elise McDaniel, and I am from Knoxville, Tennessee, and also in the FUTURE program at the University of Tennessee. So the FUTURE program introduced a pilot program of housing and now I am part of that. When I first heard of this, I started crying (happy tears). I also had mixed feelings about this. Then I started to move into my dorm. My brother, Cole, moved to Berry College, and I miss him. These are big changes in my life. Before my parents left, I started crying (sad tears). Then I got over it. Now I am independent, like calling a bus that I take every day, going to eat by myself, walking around campus, and making forward plans. I also stay involved around campus, like Boss Dance, Best Buddies, and Student Government Association. If I hadn't gone to college, I wouldn't be able to live in a dorm and live by myself. College means a lot to me. I get to take classes and internships. Lastly, I am going to get a job someday. All because of college.

Kaelan Knowles

One rough thing that happened in college was . . .

One of the rough things that happened to me in college was when I was in my conflict resolution class. We had a group project, and one of the students in my group decided to change the Google Docs PowerPoint altogether. Furthermore, this made me feel a little frustrated since she was not part of the group meetups. Soon after, I got to look over the PowerPoint and did the best I could to understand the changes she made. Before the next day, I talked with my friend, and he helped me calm down and I was able to approach her with respect.

From the Photo Essay

The following are transcripts of the handwritten text in the accompanying photo essays (Figures 18.1–18.4).

KAELAN KNOWLES

My Thoughts

1st. When I first came to college I wanted to be an animator.

2st. 2nd year, I wanted to be an international business major.
こんにちは (Hello)

3st. Still international. 日本ご (Japanese language)

4st. 한국어 (Korean language) Then my fourth year I decided to become a tutor for people in South Korea.

I say this all to say your major can change throughout college is true and you can do anything when you set your mind to it.

I chose this picture because this is me in Chattanooga and this is my first trip I planned on my own, so I say again you can do anything.

감사합니다 (Thank you)
どうもありがとございます。(And thank you very much)

Figure 18.1. Kaelan Knowles

BREANA WHITTLESEY

Hi my name is Breana Whittlesey. I go to Kennesaw State University. My major is Early Childhood Education. I graduated from KSU in 2019. I'm a junior. I have ADHD. I get a lot of help in KSU. I love working with kids. When I leave KSU I hope I become a student teacher. KSU taught me a lot for the past 3 years. I will miss everyone when I leave KSU.

Updated from Breana

Hello, my name is Breana Whittlesey. I was born in Bronx, New York. I moved a lot. I went to Kennesaw State University for four years. I loved the help Kennesaw State University helped me. I felt like I had another family with the staff.

My experience at Kennesaw State University was the best experience I had because I had the best professors and the best mentors to help me with my classes. I made a lot of great friends, and they will all be missed because I finished at Kennesaw State University because I can't go back and take classes with them again. I also got into a regular college for nursing in May.

Kennesaw State University will be missed, and all my friends I had, my teachers, and professors. I appreciated their help, even my mentors, for everything they have done for me. I try my best to come back and visit them. Hopefully, I can get a job with them some day and help other kids with disabilities.

Hi My Name is Breana Whittlesey
I go to ~~Kennss~~ Kennesaw State
university, My major is Early Childhood
Edcation, I granded from KSU in 2019
I'm a Jounior, I have ADHD, I get
alot of help in KSU, I love working
with kids. When I leave KSU I
hope I Become a Studen't teacher
KSU taught me alot for the
the past 3 years. I will miss
everyone when I leave ~~Ki~~ KSU.

Figure 18.2. Breana Whittlesey

KENNETH KELTY

This is a photo of me while at the international festival and was able to meet up with friends.

The UP Program was a fully inclusive program and campus. Near the end of my second semester I was able to convince the administration to make the schedule system more flexible because before all activities had to be planned two weeks in advance and no one plans all school activities that early. Flexibility is important.

To me college means growing and learning what you thought was not possible. Self-determination is a major about going to college.

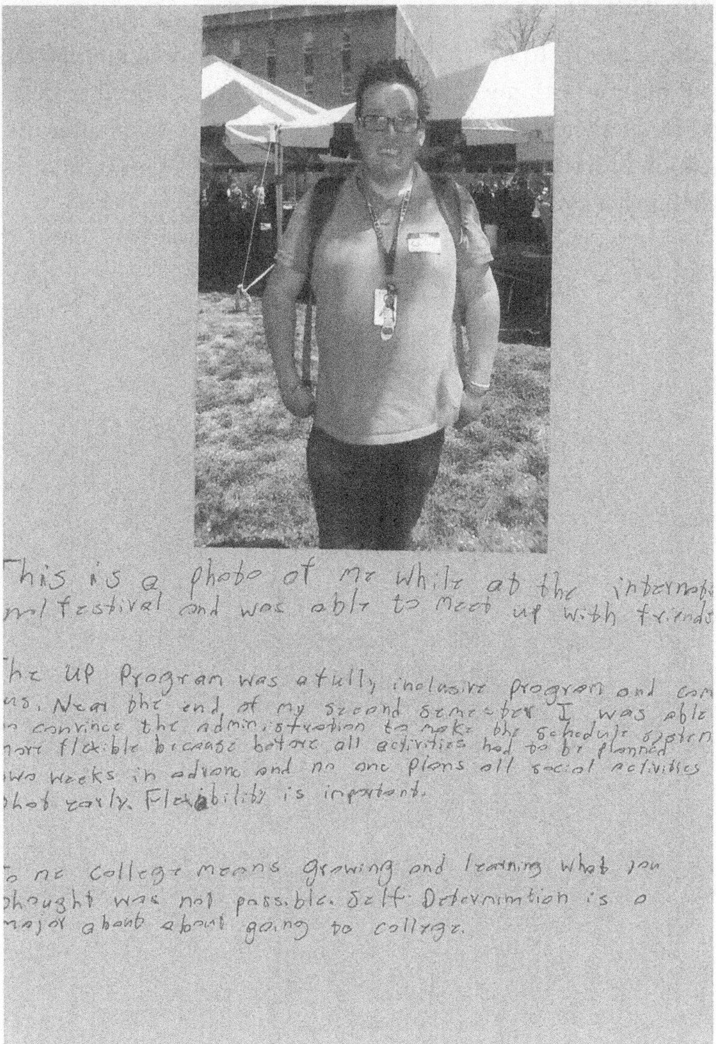

This is a photo of me while at the internati-
nal festival and was able to meet up with friends

The UP Program was a fully inclusive program and cam-
us. Near the end of my second semester I was able
to convince the administration to make the schedule system
more flexible because before all activities had to be planned
two weeks in advance and no one plans all social activities
that early. Flexibility is important.

To me college means growing and learning what you
thought was not possible. Self Determination is a
major about about going to college.

Figure 18.3. Kenneth Kelty

KATIE BARTLETT

College means to me that being more independent and having a lot of time with my family doing things. What I need to do to get ready ahead of time. Could find a job and have a better life. School. Marriage—relationships. Job. Family—kids. Guitar—worship leader.

COLLEGE
Katie
Guitar
Worship leader
College means to me that being
infentant and having a lot of time with my
Family doing things What I need to
to get ready Ahead of time could find a Job and
have a better life
School,
Malliage, - relationships

Figure 18.4. Katie Bartlett

Part III

Inclusion as Action

DIVERSIFYING STUDENT EXPERIENCES

Students with intellectual disability have been long excluded from higher education, a space that has traditionally been opened primarily through extensive privilege and based on antiquated ideas about the value of academic merit. Other groups have experienced exclusion on race, ethnicity, sexual orientation, gender identity, disability, socioeconomics, and countless other ways. What we claim here is that students with intellectual disability, just like all other people, do not have a singular identity. The nature of their disability does not negate other identities, but these identities overlap to inform a whole personhood. This section supports the understanding of diverse student experiences in inclusive higher education.

Inclusion is not something we *create* or *do* or *hope for.* Inclusion is a commitment to constant action, ingrained steadfastness, and the consistent actualization of belonging. It forces us, all of us, to question again and again the biases that we bring to our experiences. We cannot be satisfied with the progress that we have made. What lies on the horizon? What have we missed? And how can we look at our own inclusive practices from a critical lens to push ourselves, and those around us, to do better?

19

Hi, I'm Jake Miller

Jake Miller and Katie Ducett

If you have been lucky enough to spend some time in Pittsford, New York, or at Nazareth College, there is a good chance you have heard these four words, "Hi, I'm Jake Miller." As a mentor in a program called LifePrep@Naz, I heard those words for the first time in January 2015. LifePrep had only been around for almost four years at that point, and I had been working with the program for about a year and a half. Getting to know Jake Miller from that point on has been one of the best parts of my life.

Jake took this picture of us at the Nazareth College Reunion and Homecoming weekend in 2019. This event is a tradition that Jake enjoys attending every year, along with many other friends of ours.

Jake knows everyone. He is a celebrity at Nazareth College, as well as at many of the other places he frequents (Wegmans, Red Wings baseball games, and Sunshine Camp, just to name a few). You often will see Jake with a group of friends exploring a museum, eating at a restaurant, or watching a sports event. Jake and some of our mutual friends even have an annual tradition of going to Seabreeze Amusement Park every summer (even though weather and Covid-19 have put a wrench in that the last few years).

One thing that Jake loves to do often is take pictures. If you spend any time with him, there will most likely be pictures taken at least a few times throughout the adventure. Sometimes they are

Figure 19.1. Katie and Jake

selfies with Jake, but often he likes taking pictures of his friends together, as well as the environment they are in.

Throughout this chapter, Jake is hoping to share with the world some of the pictures he has taken during his years as a student and employee at Nazareth College. Along with the pictures are some pieces of writing Jake wanted to accompany his pictures. Although the writing in the following sections was physically typed into the document by Katie, it was thought up by Jake through FaceTime and text conversations. In-person connection did not happen due to Covid-19 restrictions. Jake has had full veto power over what was written, to be sure it represents his true experience.

Autism

I have autism. For me, autism means I walk around and talk to a lot of people. I ask people a lot of questions. When I am excited about something, I flap my hands and sometimes I jump up and down. With my autism, I have learned to calm down when I need to and take deep breaths. Sometimes my Apple Watch Breathe app helps me take deep breaths. Taking deep breaths is a great strategy that has helped me. Autism has helped me with college and it has helped me with my jobs. Autism did not make college or my jobs any more difficult.

LifePrep@Naz

LifePrep was an option for me when I was graduating from high school. I wanted to go to college, so I applied! To get into LifePrep, I had to fill out an application and do an interview. I was accepted! When I got into the LifePrep@Naz program, I took a tour of the campus. I started as a student in LifePrep in 2015. I took this picture of the Golisano Academic Center. This is where the main LifePrep classroom is. There are a lot of other things that happen in this building too, like yoga, a lot of Nazareth classes, and church services.

When I first started at Nazareth, I used a map to learn my way around. People did not need to help me find my way. If I needed help, I would have asked though. It is a good idea to ask for help when you need it.

Figure 19.2. Golisano Academic Center at Nazareth College

LifePrep taught me how to be independent, how to get a job, life skills (cooking, money, laundry, etc.), and job skills. The diagram below shows those different things that I needed to learn to be more independent. These different things have helped me become more independent. I still practice these different skills. These skills are important for everyone, not just people with autism.

Cooking every week was fun! We learned how to cook things

Figure 19.3. Mind map for "How to Be Independent"

like grilled cheese sandwiches, French toast, blueberry muffins, banana smoothies, chocolate chip cookies, peanut butter cookies, and fudge! Yum! Our teacher would bring the recipe and the ingredients to a dorm kitchen, and we would all work together to make the recipes.

The hardest life skill for me to learn was the difference between credit cards and debit cards. My teachers and mentors helped me with this skill. I do not use a credit card or a debit card now, but I know I could if I wanted to.

I also took Nazareth classes with other Naz students who were not in LifePrep. Some classes I remember I took were yoga, ballroom dancing, percussion for music therapy, improv, and 3D design. My favorite class was improv. I liked doing improv class because I like to act, and I got to act in that class! I like acting because

I get to do impersonations. I get to say lines from movies and books that I like. I got to help pick which classes I wanted to take while I was in LifePrep!

All over campus, I had internships every semester. I had internships in the Cafe Sorelle, the box office, the dining hall, and the mailroom. The best internships for me were in the box office and in Cafe Sorelle. In the box office, I had the responsibility of putting tickets into envelopes for customers and putting the envelopes into mailboxes. In Cafe Sorelle, I made pizzas and helped clean tables. I got to help pick which internships I had, and I do not remember having any tough moments. There was one thing I did not like at my internship. I did not like using the computers when I worked at the box office.

There were mentors at LifePrep who took me to my different Naz classes and my internships. They also helped me with my homework. They were great!

The mentors helped me with school things, and they are my friends. We would go to events on campus together, like field hockey games, basketball games, theater shows, and other things like that! They also started a Best Buddies club at Nazareth, and a lot of LifePrep students, mentors, and other Nazareth students are a part of the club. They even started a choir called the EveryBuddies that I am a part of. We perform every few months!

I like being in the EveryBuddies because I get to sing songs. I like that it is inclusive because I really enjoy making new friends. We have even been having virtual practices because of Covid-19. I am happy I get to continue being in the choir even though I have graduated.

I still stay in contact with a lot of those mentors, even though I have graduated from Nazareth and most of them have graduated too. Some older mentors even came back to see me graduate from Nazareth. It was the second year that LifePrep students walked across the stage at the Naz Commencement at the Blue Cross Arena. It is important that LifePrep students get to walk across the stage, because we finished our four years of college and our programs.

We get to walk across the stage like everyone else. A lot of people stood up and cheered when I graduated! I was so very excited!

After College . . .

One of my favorite memories at Naz actually happened after I graduated. I was working my job when all the new freshmen were arriving at Nazareth College for move-in. I met those new friends for the first time! To the new students, I said, "Hi, I'm Jake Miller. I went to Naz for four years." I like to meet new people a lot! People I meet are usually friendly and have not been mean.

I don't usually get nervous when I meet new people. I just like to introduce myself and ask the other person what they like to do. Then I like to see what we have in common! I usually try hard to remember the things I have in common with other people.

Things I ask people about to find out what we have in common:

- when their birthdays are
- what they like to do
- what sports they like to watch
- what their favorite movies are
- what their favorite colors are
- what their favorite foods are

I remember a lot of the things people say for a long time because I am pretty smart! If I see them again, I will probably ask them about the thing they told me before.

I have had two different jobs since I graduated from Nazareth. I still work at both of them. One of them is in the dining hall at Nazareth. It was easier to get this job because I worked there during one of my internships. I was good at wiping tables and helping clean around Sorelle's. Those skills helped me get my job in the dining hall.

My other job is at Wegmans. At Wegmans, I get to fold pizza boxes for the pizza station, and I get to pass out Godiva chocolates to the customers at the chocolate station. It is a good job! My

Figure 19.4. Jake outside Wegmans in Pittsford

supervisor took this picture of me with a pumpkin. I am wearing a mask because this was taken during Covid-19, and we have to wear masks to keep each other safe!

I researched jobs on Indeed to get my job at Wegmans, wrote a cover letter, completed a résumé, filled out an application, and did an interview. I do not plan to leave these jobs because I really like them. If I did have to get another job for some reason, I would ask my mom or someone I trust to help me with the cover letter and résumé. Those were the hardest parts of getting a job for me.

Figure 19.5. Otto A. Shults Community Center

My Favorite Places on Campus!

I really like taking pictures. I take them all the time. Pictures are like memories of things I have done. Sometimes I show my friends and my mom my pictures to show them what things I have done. They enjoy looking at the pictures, too!

In Shults, I like the swimming pool, racquetball courts, and

Figure 19.6. Golisano Training Center

the gymnasium. I also like the bookstore where people go and buy all different types of Nazareth apparel. My favorite Naz apparel are my T-shirt and my hat. My favorite thing to do at Shults is I like to eat lunch at the Cab. The Cab is really called the Cabaret, but everyone on campus calls it the Cab. It is a café where many students and faculty get lunch or dinner. I like to go there with my friends.

At the new Golisano Training Center, I like the new indoor

Figure 19.7. Lourdes Dining Hall

track, fitness center, indoor turf, and exercise rooms. I like to play sports there that Best Buddies does for inclusive intramurals called Featured Flyers. My favorite sports to play with Featured Flyers are basketball, tennis, and softball. My favorite thing to do there is get a snack from the concession stand.

At the Lourdes Dining Hall, I like to have lunch with my LifePrep friends for $5 Fridays. One of my favorite memories is the all-you-can-eat buffets. I would go through the line and get whatever I want. My favorite thing to do is working there as a culinary ambassador. I walk around and talk to people when I work at the dining hall.

I hope that people reading this chapter learn how I was a student at Nazareth and then was able to get different jobs I enjoy!

That's it!

20

"BGWYN" and "Confidence with Curves"

Taylor Cathey

BGWYN

Every Black Woman has a story.
Nina Simone sung her song of four women with black skin,
Peaches, Sarah, Saffronia, Sweet Thing.
My name must be added to the song.
Because if I hear, "BLACK GIRL WHAT'S YOUR NAME?!"
one more time it's not going to end well.
Every time I hear "BLACK GIRL WHAT'S YOUR NAME?!"
Hold up, do you know who you are talking to?
Only badgering for the accolade.
Look at this face and mind,
The crown is what makes my presence,
Dark Chocolate dipped in Gold,
A Goddess walking the earth with greatness in a step,
Not one to provoke,
I spit bars wrapped in Silk Glitter Smoke,
The knowledge I possess will leave you woke.
I live to see a shining crown on another curly, braided mind.
Heal wounds, turn tragedy into triumph.
I can be anything because I know who I am and I don't dim the
light that shines from within.
Look at the gold trail, they're following because I'm the truth.
Nina is looking down from heaven right now,

"I saved my best for last. The worth of all of our sistahs is
complete.
My sistah tell us what your name is?"
I am Magik.

Confidence with Curves

My favorite experience on Roberts Wesleyan College campus was when I auditioned to be a model in a club fashion show. I was in chapel with my peer mentor Katelyn Ireland when we met a leader of the club SMAC (Student Multicultural Advisory Council). She was hosting auditions for their fashion show. Katelyn immediately asked the leader to add me to the list of contestants. One of my childhood dreams has always been to be a part of the fashion industry as a model or fashion designer. I was excited, and Katelyn was happy to help me too. My dream was finally coming true. I walked around with a smile on my face. On my way out of a class, I grabbed the flyer and put it into my portfolio, slowly a nasty childhood insecurity unmasked itself. My weight.

I was known for drawing clothes, not modeling them. For a long time, I kept the part about modeling a secret because I was bullied for being a heavy-set girl. The idea about being on stage in front of lots of people made me question my decision. Plus-size women were breaking barriers in the world of fashion and beauty, but maybe I didn't have what it took to be one of them. I was no Ashley Graham or Danielle Brooks. I sat and thought for a few hours about the decision. So, I chose to ask to be a host if I couldn't model. My mom told me to give it a shot and do it for myself no matter what. I took a deep breath and continued with my plans.

On a cold February afternoon, I walked the long way to the lounge across the street. I walked in, introduced myself, and told them choices. *"Oh, I'm sorry the host was already chosen. So do you just want to model?"* I said okay and set my things down. I chose my song and strutted down the long line and gave them all of me. I swung my hair, I bent over, struck my best poses, and did it with a smile. They were impressed. I felt my heart beat out of my chest.

March had arrived. Every Wednesday through Thursday night it was practice night. I made sure to bring the energy and work hard. I brought clothes to wear and planned my songs ahead of time. When I practiced my moves, I became a version of myself I didn't know I had in me. Katelyn and Rose, my mentors, were there to cheer me on. The fashion show was the night of my twenty-fourth birthday. It made it ten times more special.

The next week I was going to meet the designer I was chosen for. I couldn't wait to see what I'd be modeling in.

Unfortunately, the fashion show didn't happen. The campus was shut down due to Covid-19. Although I didn't get to walk the catwalk, I was proud of myself and everyone for the work we put in. I can look back on this experience and say I took a chance. I also left a great impression. If an opportunity like this is handed to me again, I'll surely take it.

Curves and all.

21

Inclusive College Education

Micah Gray, with Karlee Lambert and Lydia Newnum

	Stories I Can Tell about This Area
☑ Career	Paleontology/music class
☑ Academic	Test-taking skills, graduating
☑ Personal	Living in the dorm with a roommate
☑ Social	Gospel choir
☑ Other	Organization (keeping a calendar)

Figure 21.1. Micah's plan for writing this essay.

Karlee Lambert and Lydia Newnum: How have paleontology and music class helped prepare you for future jobs?

Micah Gray: When I originally came to Appalachian State University, my major was paleontology. After I started taking classes, I decided I wanted to change my major to music because I want to be a choir director. Even though I changed my major, I think paleontology has helped me prepare for a real-life work experience. This summer I was supposed to travel with my Finding Fossil Friday Group to Colorado to get a full experience of digging for fossils, but unfortunately, it got postponed due to the pandemic. My music class has helped me prepare for when I want to start and form my own choir after I graduate from college. There were so many words that I didn't know or have not heard of before; now that I know what they mean, I can't wait to use them in the future. My music professor has offered me accommodations to help me in the class and to prepare me for my future as a choir director. For example, whenever it came time to present projects, my professor would put me into a small group to present in order to make me feel more comfortable. From having this accommodation, I am able to participate in class, but to an extent that works best for me.

KL and LN: How have your test-taking skills improved? How has this helped you? How has the Scholars with Diverse Abilities Program (SDAP) prepared you for graduation?

MG: Since coming to college, my test-taking skills have improved a lot. Before college, I was struggling to make a passing grade on my tests. It seems like I'm doing much better; I'm getting higher grades on each assessment that I take. I believe that I have improved my test-taking skills through studying my materials for classes more and by having awesome student supports. Student supports are some of my fellow students that help me with things like schoolwork, notes, and assessments. My student support helps me with reading my material, as well as breaking down questions for me when I have a hard time understanding. I have benefited from having student support because they have helped in teaching me more efficient ways to study and take tests. The Scholars with Diverse Abilities Program has taught me time management and work ethic, along with more skills. Although SDAP is an academic program, I have learned a lot of life skills through my college experience.

KL and LN: What happened in the dorm? How was it living with a roommate? Do you think you're more mature from this experience?

MG: I lived in Summit Hall in the fall of 2019 and half of the spring of 2020. I really liked living in the dorm because I had the experience of living away from home for the first time. Although I really liked the dorm, I missed my family every day; one word to describe how I felt is *tragic.* I had a rough relationship with my roommate. We didn't agree on much; for example, we would argue about whether the window should be open or closed. I would say that living in the dorm made me more mature. I learned how to handle conflict with others more effectively and I learned how to go about fulfilling my responsibilities on my own.

KL and LN: How has gospel choir helped you, or how has it improved your social skills?

MG: To preface, I have a big passion for singing and for being in the choir. Gospel choir has given me the opportunity to come together in a group, to make new friends, and it has helped me become more comfortable with performing in front of large crowds. Gospel choir has also made me become more involved with my church. Church means a lot to me, so being more involved has been really meaningful.

KL and LN: How has transitioning from in-person classes to online made you feel in light of the pandemic?

MG: At first, when we had to move out of our dorms and leave campus, I was upset because I felt my full college experience was cut short. I was not used to online Zoom classes at first when we transitioned, but doing Zoom throughout the day and the week made me feel more comfortable because I began getting used to using Zoom. My paleontology class in person was enjoyable because I felt I could learn about different rocks through seeing it in person through my professor. I struggled with the course online at the beginning but learned how to adapt based on the format of the course. I became more on top of things because I was able to break down more information on my own time; I did this by keeping a schedule and constantly going over it throughout the day to make sure I was completing all of my assignments. My transition as far as my

2020 semester has been well. I feel more comfortable doing online than in person due to the pandemic.

KL and LN: How did you learn to maintain a calendar? How has keeping a calendar helped you in school and in life?

MG: My mom was the main person that taught me how to maintain a calendar. She taught me what things should go into the calendar, such as due dates for assignments. In high school, I had a planner; I kept track of important dates, such as field trips, tests, and birthdays. To me, keeping a calendar is very important because it helps me to remember things that I need to do, like attending doctors' appointments. Keeping a calendar has helped me a lot throughout my college journey. I have all of my class times programmed into Google Calendar so that I never forget to attend a class. My calendar also helps me in school because, since I have my class times logged, I know when I can commit to other responsibilities.

KL and LN: Regarding the previous chart, how did you use the chart as an organizational tool to complete this essay?

MG: The chart helped me organize my thoughts in a visual, central location. I was able to group my thoughts into rows and columns, which ultimately helped me to further breakdown my ideas for this essay. My student supports asked me what I think about when I hear the words *career, academic, social, personal,* and *other.* The first thought that popped into my head when I thought about *career* was paleontology and music. I thought about paleontology and music because the word *career* means "job." I am very interested in paleontology, but I am studying music to help me in my future career. As far as academics, I thought about test-taking skills and my future graduation. We used this same process throughout the entirety of the chart.

22

My UC Perspective

Joshua R. Hourigan

My name is Joshua Hourigan, and I'm a TAP student from Muncie, Indiana. TAP is an acronym that stands for the Transition and Access Program at the University of Cincinnati (UC). This program focuses on employment skills, independent living, social and engagement skills, and having the full four-year experience. It's an educational program that involves creating a living-learning opportunity that builds career skills, academic achievements, independent living, social networks, and a bright future.

My time at UC is with no doubt a wonderful experience. Living in the residence halls feels so cozy and relaxing with the campus view on the hall floors. I absolutely love getting to know the diverse and inclusive student population, particularly when I was at the TAP Summer Orientation Workshop. In the summer orientation, it's the time where the new incoming freshmen are required to stay for June and July summer sessions on campus for a week to get situated with getting around on campus, living in the dorms overnight, learning the curriculum, and participating in a traditional orientation assembly. It made me feel a little bit nervous because I've never been there before and I hardly knew anybody, but as I started getting to know everyone, I felt pretty welcome there. The opportunities and the UC traditions are endless.

Some of my favorite student organizations that I've got the chance to be in are the UC Bearcat Jazz Ensemble as a percussionist; the UC Hepcat Swing Dancing Club to learn traditional and modern swing dances; and the UC Hillel Jewish Student Center for social activities, Jewish holidays, and being the volunteer coordinator for Challah for Hunger, which is an organization in which we bake and sell challah bread to raise social awareness and to raise money for organizations to end hunger worldwide. These organizations are so important to me because it helps me build social relationships with peers and engage directly with other people. And Hillel is also important to me because I want to preserve my tradition, participate in some congregational settings, and meet other Jewish people that share similar cultures. And last October, I had the honor to appear on Channel 12 to talk about my experience. I was picked because the people at Advancement and Transition Services (ATS) thought that I would be the perfect person to talk about what college is like for me, and I told them about how this program is changing my life. They showed this on TV because the reporters wanted to prove that college is an option for students like me. It was unforgettable the way that the news anchors asked me lot of questions about my overall experience, and we joked around quite a bit when we were on the air too!

Academically, my professors and teachers are amazing at what they do. On a daily basis at the Teacher's College Building, I've been learning a lot of stuff, including time management, vocational exploration, academic support, developing relationships with my peers, and how to succeed in life. Additionally, the TAP student leaders are always there to help me with some personal goals, managing my stress, and making sure that I thrive and flourish throughout the year. Plus, they help me with developing some skills that will help me with things to help self-monitor and to try some stress relievers as well. To manage my stress, I either pace outside of the halls or sometimes pace outside the dorm rooms to let all of the stress out, and it usually works for me most of the time. A life coach is always there for me if I need some help with my goals, and we usually sit and talk about what my goals should be for every week. Also, there are some awesome academic coaches that help me with my academics, staying organized, and keeping up with my tasks. Occasionally during academic support, the homework can be challenging depending on the class, subject, or topic, but luckily I have a professor or an academic coach to ask for help if needed. In every spring, UC's ATS has the opportunity to have a special fundraiser event at the Fifth Third Arena to raise money for those amazing programs at UC.

I've had so much support from my friends, family, and relatives throughout the year, and it makes me feel proud of myself for what I'm accomplishing. My hopes and dreams by the time I graduate from TAP are that I have good quality of life, have a productive job, have a healthy lifestyle, continue developing my social skills with others, live on my own, and am able to have the skills to succeed in life with so many chances in reach. And I hope to see what my potential has in store for me for the years to come to have a true purpose in my life.

23

Phoenix Nation as in Spirit

Cleo Hamilton

My name is Cleo Hamilton. I graduated in 2020 from Syracuse University with a certificate in sports management. I am from Syracuse, New York. I am currently interning in the Office of Alumni Engagement on campus. Some of the things I do during my internship include reviewing the Office of Alumni Engagement's Instagram projects, assisting in creating and participating in the Orange Central 2020 video, and helping to manage and distribute materials for Orange Central 2020. Throughout my internship, I felt very connected to the staff within the Office of Alumni Engagement and felt that my work was valued.

One thing people notice about me is how much I love Syracuse University (SU). I am always wearing SU colors. During my four years on campus, I participated in a wide variety of events, clubs, and organizations. I will write a little about what I did on campus and share some pictures of my experience. I am very active on social media, always posting pictures. There was an article I published with Beth Myers and Katherine Vroman that uses my Facebook posts to talk about my first two years of college. If you want to follow me, you can follow me @realbronzeyellowphoenix25. I picked out photographs that tell a little about my college experience.

One of the first things I did on campus was participate in the OttoTHON, a dance marathon that supports Upstate Golisano

Figure 23.1. A group of students smiling at OttoTHON

Children's Hospital. Here is a picture of my team at OttoTHON (Figure 23.1). In my junior year, I raised over $900 through social media. This made me feel happy that I could make a difference. From my sophomore to senior year, I was part of the Morale Dance Committee as part of OttoTHON. In my senior year, I was the morale captain for the committee. I was also part of the eboard for OttoTHON.

A couple of other things I did during my time at SU include Relay for Life. I participated in Relay for Life for three years. Each year we would do a twelve-hour walking event to raise money. I was the recruitment chair and I sent emails to other students to get them to participate. I felt it was important not only to join Relay for Life but also to get others to participate in it because it helps people. Relay for Life also gave me another opportunity to be connected on campus.

I was the first InclusiveU student to participate in the student government association at SU. It was important for me to be involved in the student government association at SU because it gave me the opportunity to help other SU students and student organizations. Being the first InclusiveU student to join the student government association at SU helped give representation to all SU students. When I joined the Student Association, I participated in weekly meetings, and sometimes the student newspaper would report on our meetings. I was interviewed for different articles in the student newspaper, including one about World Autism Awareness Day (Myelle Lansat, "SU Students Continue the Dialogue Ahead of World Autism Awareness Day," *Daily Orange,* April 2, 2018, http://dailyorange.com/2018/04/su-students-continue-dialogue-ahead-world-autism-awareness-day/). In this article, I talk about how I have a positive attitude and want to succeed.

I also traveled with people from InclusiveU to Washington, D.C., to speak at a screening on the film *Intelligent Lives*. This is a picture of me wearing a suit looking out over a lobby in the Senate. Many people have told me that they like this picture of me (Figure 23.2). In D.C., we talked to alumni of SU. I talked to senators and other people about college. I also spoke at the State of the Art Conference in Reno.

One of the best things that happened to me while I was a student at SU was being chosen as a Remembrance Scholar ("History," Remembrance, Syracuse University, https://remembrance.syr.edu/about/). The scholar program is dedicated to the thirty-five SU students who died as part of the bombing of Pan Am Flight 103 on December 21, 1988. My friend Tori was a Remembrance Scholar during my sophomore year. She invited me to a candlelight vigil as part of the Remembrance Week. In the following year, I attended the rose-laying ceremony. I decided to apply for the scholar program. I worked hard on my application, and I was picked. This is a picture of me and the fellow scholars (Figure 23.3).

Figure 23.2. Cleo looking out over a lobby in the Senate while wearing a suit

This is an article my friend Karly wrote about me and the Remembrance Scholar program: Karly Grifasi, "Remembrance Scholar Cleo Hamilton Exemplifies Student Leadership and Commitment," Syracuse University News, Campus & Community, May 31, 2019, https://news.syr.edu/blog/2019/05/31/remembrance-scholar-cleo-hamilton-exemplifies-student-leadership-and-commitment/.

When I found out I was chosen to be a Remembrance Scholar, I was shocked and happy. Being a Remembrance Scholar meant that I was one of only thirty-five students to be selected. I was also the first InclusiveU student to be selected. It was important

Figure 23.3. Cleo and fellow Remembrance Scholars

to me to be chosen as a Remembrance Scholar because it meant that I was really a part of the SU community.

I have had so many opportunities to participate in organizations, attend events, and meet people at Syracuse. I am very happy with my decision to go to Syracuse. To me, Syracuse University is the best university out there. Since I graduated from InclusiveU, I have been working and am planning for my future, where I hope to move to Brooklyn and become a sports photographer. I feel I am ready for this after my time at InclusiveU at Syracuse University.

24

My Excel Story

George Barham

When I first joined Georgia Tech Excel, I was more excited than nervous. I got to join different clubs at Georgia Tech. First, I did some improv at DramaTech. Then I assisted children with playing soccer in the GOALS club. I also meet up with the Runnin' Wreck to do some street running on Monday, Wednesday, and Friday evenings. And my most personal favorite club that I participated in was called ORGT, which stands for Outdoor Recreation Georgia Tech. The trips I did were cascading, which is the opposite of rock climbing, where you climb down a waterfall, caving horizontal and vertical (that's where I got a chance to explore caves), and bikepacking where I carry packs and camping equipment with my bike and go camping. One of my favorite parts in Excel was learning how to use the computer graphic app called Maya. I used it in an inclusive class called Construct-Moving Image. I learned how to make modeled shapes, size them up, move them around, twirl them, and give them brighter or darker colors. My final project in that class was a group project where we developed a video game that takes place in a space mansion where every room is based on what the planet/god/goddess represents. For instance, Mercury, the messenger god, was the library and Neptune, god of the sea, was the bathroom. And now I've used it to make a model of Buzz, the yellowjacket mascot, by using poly model shapes, making them bigger, smaller, taller, shorter, thinner, and wider. And I rendered the colors to make them brighter or darker. I also loved being camp counselor at the Excel Summer Academy. We got to come up with ideas for upgrading attractions at the Georgia Aquarium. Another one of my favorite Excel events was Six Flags Night, where we got to ride on our favorite rides. My other favorite part was when I went to the water park hotel, the Great Wolf Lodge, with my friends. I also learned how to host events like movie nights, drawing clubs, and dance events. The Excel Program has shown me how to make friends, like the Smith brothers, who invited me to a fun trip at the water park, Great Wolf Lodge, and my friend Antonio, who invited me and four other Excel friends to Disneyland next holiday season. Excel also brought me on a tour at Warner Broadcasting, formerly Turner Broadcasting, and from the moment I first stepped in there it felt like my dream place. That is when I knew that I wanted to pursue animation for my career. I love animated television shows. I will do this by taking additional online trainings to improve my animation skills, especially in the Maya and Unity programs.

25

#CreatingMyOwnLife

Payton Storms

Believe in yourself and all that you are. Know that there is something inside you that is greater than any obstacle.
—*Christian D. Larson*

Everyone always said to me that college is the best time of your life. You make your own schedule of things that you want to do. There is nobody creating your life for you. The first thing I thought when I got to college was, "This is the first day of the rest of my life. I get to make my own decisions now." My first instinct was not to let go of childhood. I haven't introduced myself yet. My name is Payton Storms, and I go to the University of Kansas (KU).

I was raised in a small town in Kansas, and moving to a bigger city was a big change for me. I saw a lot of growth in myself once I made the transition. I was a shy, introverted eighteen-year-old. I definitely changed in a big way once I started making friends and getting out of my comfort zone.

The things that I am now responsible for in order to take care of myself are things like education and meals. I have to pick out my own outfits. Health care is a big problem right now because not a lot of people have good health care during coronavirus.

I go to the store with my mom, and she helps me shop and get healthy foods. I would buy a bunch of junk food and not eat very healthy without help. I go to get groceries every two weeks. I cook my own food and eat leftovers for a week. My roommates and I normally eat by ourselves. I am getting myself up and getting myself to and from classes. I have some trouble getting to class on time sometimes, but that is Monday's fault.

When I lived at home, I had to get a ride from my parents. We lived half an hour away from the Lawrence campus. Now I live five minutes away from campus. It is much closer of a distance than when I lived at home with my parents. The bus system was one of the things that I figured out all on my own. For transportation, I had to figure out how to take the bus and where they drop off. Sometimes I walk, but there are times that I need the bus, and they are really handy. There are three buses that I take to get to the places that I need to go.

Once I got to KU, I moved and everything. I started getting on different buses to learn where they go so if I ever needed to find a specific place, I knew which bus to get on. I use the Lawrence bus app on my phone to get around and to find out how fast they will be getting to me. I have helped other people find their way around. Like, there was one person who wanted to know the closest bus stop to Target, so I told him what stop to get off at.

The summer before college started is when I started to meet people in the program. It was over Zoom meetings because the coronavirus pandemic started during my spring break of high school. Covid broke free, and it started in China. It seemed like the world was ending, but I was given hope. Since I was shy, I didn't want to come out of my shell and talk to people. Once I got to campus, I really opened myself to new experiences. I made more friendships.

The first week of college, when we were getting to know our little group of Transition to Postsecondary Education students here at KU, I met a friend; her name is Nicole. She and her sister had just moved into a townhouse, and they had one extra spare bedroom. I needed somewhere else to live besides my parents' basement, so I moved in with them. Getting used to living with people that are not family members was a little bit of an adjustment. I didn't do so well with the last couple of house changes.

I was in the foster care system for two and a half years, and I moved houses a lot when I was younger, so I got used to living with someone that I didn't know. When I was six years old, I moved to Basehor, Kansas, with my sister who was eight years old. We got adopted when I was in second grade and she was in fourth. I remember that day like it was yesterday. I have this quote from Theodor Seuss Geisel that I try to live by: "When something bad happens, you have three choices: You can either let it define you, let it destroy you, or let it strengthen you." I have loved that quote since I was a little kid. I think in this home, I am here to stay, and I have never felt so at home here than I am now.

Since I am only part-time in this program, I have more time for fun clubs and activities. I am already in a club, the KU Fun Club. It is a club that goes and does fun things together. Like they go and get coffee at McLain's Market, a go-to spot for breakfast, lunch, dinner, and drinks, or go to football games together. I have not gone and hung out with them yet, but they meet every Monday. I have been too busy with school and schoolwork. They go somewhere and play Dungeons and Dragons. The student union activities are a lot of fun to go to. There are movie nights, bingo nights with food, and outdoor activities like dances and other fun things.

I also have a really fun peer mentor. Her name is Katy, and she likes to go get coffee a lot. Personally, I don't like coffee; I am more of a tea drinker. Her major is pre-nursing. We do a lot of things together. We have gone to the park together, eaten ice cream together, and walked the streets of downtown together. The week before our next meeting, we plan out the next thing that we will do.

My parents and I have a changing relationship that is turning into a friendship. I still don't think that my dad has made the transition. Every time I see him, he still treats me as if I never left the house, reminding me of things I already know. I think that once he starts to see me as an adult, then our friendship will change and be different. He won't be telling me what to do anymore. I don't know when he'll see me as an adult, maybe when I am out of college. Maybe when I grow up and get married. I don't know.

I am taking two classes since I am part-time here. One of my classes is career-based. I am learning about things that you have to have before getting a job, like a résumé and good references. The other class is learning about the college.

I did a lot of planning for my future here at KU. I always wanted to be a Jayhawk. Now that I am, it is super exciting. I am looking forward to taking a journalism class in the spring semester. I am really interested in this class because I love to write. I found my love for writing in eighth grade when I started to write a book of my own about my life, like a biography. I am almost done with that one. Now I just have to get people to edit it for me and help me publish it.

In my spare time, I just watch Netflix. Right now, I have a few shows I am in the middle of. They are called *Riverdale, Gilmore Girls,* and *Sister, Sister.* I would love a job as a librarian because I like to read also, so I could check out a couple of books; also, I just need some cash. My dream job would be as a computer help assistant or something because I am a great help when someone has trouble with something on any electronic device.

Navigating trying to find a job in this pandemic is hard in itself. I am turning in several job applications, and not one single job has called me back. I have applied to a bunch of places, like grocery stores, auto parts stores, and restaurants. I applied all on my own. Now I am working with my career adviser to help polish my résumé and work on my cover letter.

College is the best time of my life right now. You get to be your own kind of person; there's nobody that is making your decisions for you. My first instinct when I got here was to not let go of childhood. The moment my parents left, I was an adult that had to figure something out by myself.

26

Inclusive College Education

Makayla Adkins

As a student at Appalachian State and being in the Scholars with Diverse Abilities Program (SDAP), my best experience is making friends and being able to live together and being more independent. I find it easy to live with them. We all get along and we communicate very well with each other. Being in this program has helped me to make new friends and has helped me with being responsible. For example, I learned how to manage money this year by tracking what I spent and what I earned. It has helped me to figure out when to eat, especially with getting together with my friends to go out. SDAP has helped me to be more social, not just by making friends in the dorm but by making friends outside of the dorm as well. With SDAP, it has made living with my suitemates and roommates a lot easier. It has also helped to be confident and more outgoing.

I can say that there is a difference in living at home versus living with my friends or on campus. I feel more independent and can take care of myself and make my own plans without needing any help. I think living with my friends is a lot more fun, especially over the weekends. We like to get together and figure out what we could do over the weekend, or sometimes we just stay in the dorm and watch movies or sit around on our phones or just have interesting conversations. Sometimes we walk around campus at night or stop by Insomnia, which is a cookie and ice cream place near campus. What I like most about being with my friends is that we all have a lot of things in common. I think that makes it a little bit easier to live together. The other thing that makes it easier is that we get along very well with each other; if there is an issue, then we all talk about it to get it figured out. Or if someone is needing help, it could be with an assignment or just help with taking out their trash, we all pitch in to help sometimes or just one person helps. And if any of us needs help with schoolwork, there is at least one person willing to help while the rest of us can give our opinions if needed. My friends also help me to stay on track and not get distracted.

I really enjoy living in the dorm, but living in the dorm means that I have to live with other people. Sometimes with that there are things that I don't like, since my roommate and suitemates have long hair and with that comes hair being all over the floor and sometimes in the shower and in my room. When I walk around with my socks on, the hair gets caught in my socks, and sometimes there will be hair somewhere on me that isn't mine. I like living with my friends, but I also have pet peeves. We all do, and we sometimes talk about how much hair is on the floor and how we can prevent the hair from getting everywhere. Or we talk about whose turn it is to clean certain places in the bathroom or whose turn it is to buy toilet tissue. We try to communicate that as much as possible; that way it doesn't turn into an argument or a problem. I also enjoy living in the new dorms. Compared to last year living in Summit, the dorms in Thunder Hill are a lot nicer. But there have been a few problems that have happened with the dorms like mice, mold, and Covid.

Sometimes I do wish the construction would stop all together as well; that way we don't have to deal with the construction workers still working on some parts of our new dorms. They didn't really make sure everything was up to code. They built this building within a matter of a few months, which can also be a bit tricky because sometimes either the construction workers or it could be just the wiring that triggers the fire alarm more than usual. And we've had a few problems with the elevators not working most of the time. They are still working on some of the cracks that are in the wall because, like I said before, they built this building within a matter of a few months. You will start to see huge cracks in the wall that they have to fix, or if paint is chipping off the wall, they also have to fix it. I just wish they would have taken their time with building the dorms instead of rushing everything.

I enjoy living on campus because the one thing I like about it is my job that I have. I'm working at the Student Recreation Center, which is on the other side of campus kind of where my dorm is. I like working there because the people are very kind and hardworking, and they are willing to help if I have any questions about anything involving my job. I ask questions about sanitizing because that's part of my job. I sanitize the weight equipment and the machines. The other part of my job is that I make sure everyone is following the safety guidelines with the gym and with Covid. The only part I don't really like about my job is that I have to stand there from 6:00 p.m. to 10:15 p.m. on Mondays and on Tuesdays 8:00 p.m. to 10:00 p.m., which isn't that bad, but watching people to make sure they are following the rules or if they need a certain type of equipment, such as resistance bands or the muscle rollers or a weightlifting belt, can be kind of difficult at some point. We are limited to certain types of equipment, so it makes it a bit harder when someone walks up to the desk and asks for something that's not there anymore. I also had two campus jobs, but I was forced to quit the other job, which was working at the dining hall on campus, because there were a high number of Covid cases. I had to quit, or they were forced to let me go. I didn't do anything bad; they didn't want to risk losing their staff because they are short on staff, and they didn't want them getting sick from the college students working there. They let most of the college students go, but at least I applied for two jobs because if I didn't, I wouldn't have a job right now. I really have enjoyed my college experience, and I will definitely miss being around college students and just college in general.

27

My Story about Aggies Elevated at Utah State University

Brenna Mantz Nielsen

My story begins of how Aggies Elevated was a good program to help me get an education and a job at the Center for Persons with Disabilities. I have been in Aggies Elevated for two years. This program has helped me gain my independence by living on my own and helped me to succeed. I was able to take awesome classes and make new friends. The classes I took my first year in this program were Career Exploration, Strategies for Reading, University Connections, and Strategies for Academic Success for my first semester. My favorite class of that semester was the Strategies for Reading because I got taught how to have better writing skills and got to read good books. For the spring semester of 2016, the classes I took were Health and Wellness, Career Exploration Part 2, Country Swing Dance, Self-Determination, and a swimming class. For this semester, my favorite class had to be Self-Determination, because it helped me to learn skills to help gain confidence to become independent on my own.

The second year I was in Aggies Elevated was good and also a little rocky. There were some experiences I had to deal with in my personal life and school life at the same time. The classes were a little more challenging. The classes I took for my first semester of my second year were Introduction to Writing, Family Finance, Basketball, Career-Related Social Skills, and Work Internship.

My favorite class was Career-Related Social Skills because I learned how to be a good employee at any place I worked at in the future. The skills I learned from this class include how to behave and act in a workplace. Also, to know the policies that need to be obeyed in a workplace at all times. It was a good class to have in this program to help me have the skills I need for the future so I can continue being successful. My last semester, the classes I took were Rape Aggression Defense, Navigating Adulthood, Work Internship, and Interpersonal Communication. My favorite class from my last semester was Work Internship because I enjoyed getting the job skills I need to have in any office job I wanted. I worked at an assisted living place for older adults, and it was called Terrace Grove. I enjoyed that because I got to do different office tasks and learn the basics and help the people if they needed anything. I really enjoyed doing that.

I had mentors I worked with who became my really good friends, and I let them know how I am doing. I got along with my mentors because they helped me learn skills that can help me in my future career, social, and personal life. They taught me how to create boundaries and helped me come up with goals that needed to be achieved. What I liked about Aggies Elevated is I got to learn skills that can help me do well in a job that I want. Also, I loved how the program was created and how it's helpful to help people with disabilities to get a job and also go back to college. I liked how I had help to find the skills that I needed to have to learn to become an independent woman. The skills I learned were how to make boundaries, social skills, and job skills that are good in the working field. I also found out who I was and learned to become successful in life. I made good memories when I was in this program and kept doing the best I can. The memorable thing I had was that there was a time when a professor helped me with my assignment that was really hard to understand. I asked her if she could clarify what I needed to know about the essay in order to get a good grade in her class. She gave me suggestions on what would be easy for me to understand the instructions of how she wanted this essay written. It was a good experience. I learned from that it's okay to ask for help when things are hard to understand.

I put a lot of effort into becoming successful and not letting the hard times get to me. I am grateful that I made friends in this program, and they were there for me in the hard times. I am still friends with these wonderful people and hang out with them occasionally. I am grateful that I learned boundaries and how to stand up for myself. The example I have is that there were fellow students who made me feel uncomfortable on certain things. I had to create boundaries on them because there are some things and situations that don't need to become a big deal. I did not want people to know about personal things going on in my life. I enjoyed learning how to get the job skills that I needed so I can prepare for the career I want. I still have those skills I learned, and I use them in my daily life. The example I want to share is that the current job I am working at is at Utah State University. I am a receptionist in the Child Care Nutrition Program at the Center for Persons with Disabilities. I also help different departments with their office work as well. I help with the Up to 3 Program, Technical Assistance for Excellence in Special Education, and the business office by helping with different office tasks that need to get completed. I enjoy working at Utah State University because I love doing office work and I work with wonderful people.

Aggies Elevated is a good program to help young adults who have disabilities and want to be treated like other people and to get a chance to get an education and job-training skills. I really am grateful for the people who were in charge of this program and taught me how I can be independent and stay positive every day. I felt really excited that I am a successful adult and I keep smiling. I am happy to remember the good things and how beneficial this program was for me. I enjoyed learning how to get the job skills that I needed so I can prepare for the career I want. I still have those skills I learned and use them in my daily life. I am glad I have chosen this program to help me come so far and overcome so many obstacles. Aggies Elevated has been a great program to be in, and it helped me achieve the dreams I was able to reach for.

28

Questions and Answers

Lawrence Sapp

Question: What's the name of the college that you attend?

Lawrence Sapp: University of Cincinnati [UC].

Question: Did you look at other colleges?

LS: Yes.

Question: Why did you choose the University of Cincinnati?

LS: Because I liked the campus, it was a big school, they had a good swim team.

Question: Was this an easy or difficult decision?

LS: Kind of hard. I looked at other schools too, but this ended up being the best for me.

Question: What year are you in college?

LS: Freshman.

Question: Do you live on campus?

LS: Yes. In a dorm.

Question: Can you tell us more about your dorm?

LS: My dorm is very nice. I live in a two-bedroom suite with four other guys. There's a laundry room downstairs where I can use my Bearcat card to pay to use the machines. I have my own mailbox and I get an email whenever there are packages waiting for me at the front desk.

Question: Is this your first time living away from home?

LS: Yes.

Question: How has this experience been for you?

LS: It's been a lot of fun. I've traveled with swimming away from home before, so this wasn't hard for me.

Question: What is good about living at college?

LS: I can go wherever I want. I make a lot of friends and meet lots of new people.

Question: What is difficult about living at college?

LS: Sometimes I have to see the same people a lot.

Question: What are some things that you like to do when you're not in class?

LS: You can walk or skateboard around campus. You can play football with friends, go to restaurants, go shopping, go to parties, make dates. I like video race car games.

Question: How are classes going for you?

LS: I am doing good. The last week in August I went to real classes on Wednesday and Friday. [Online classes] are so boring; they are stressful. Covid makes you stay away from people. I want harder classes, a higher level next year. I work hard, focus on classes, on school, study, and do my homework.

Question: Can you tell us more about your classes?

LS: I take some classes in person and some on my computer.

Question: You mention that you want harder classes and a higher level next year. Did you get to pick your classes this year or did someone else choose them for you?

LS: I chose the classes, but because of the program that I'm in, I have to choose from some of those classes.

Question: Why do you think they are too easy? Are they regular college classes or specialized classes only for students in your program?

LS: Most classes are only for students in my program.

Question: What classes would you like to take instead?

LS: I want to take more classes with other students at the school so that I feel like I'm really part of the college.

Question: Do you feel like you're being included with the other college students?

LS: Yes.

Question: What kinds of things do you do with other college students?

LS: I eat and hang out with them at restaurants and other activities.

Question: Do you take classes with them? If so, which ones?

LS: No, I don't take classes with them, but I want to.

Question: Do you live with them or only with students from your program?

LS: Only students from my program.

Question: Do you go to parties with them?

LS: Because of coronavirus, there aren't lots of parties, but they do invite me places.

Question: Are you in clubs and organizations with other college students?

LS: Yes, the swim club, and I played flag football.

Question: What do you like about being at the University of Cincinnati?

LS: I like the campus, a new place. I like to walk around campus or ride my skateboard. I like making new friends.

Question: What don't you like about being at the University of Cincinnati?

LS: I am pretty disappointed that sports aren't on. Everyone hates Covid; the goal is just to hang on until it goes away.

There's no training until next semester. Some of my swimmer friends are pretty sad.

Question: You're an amazing swimmer and on the U.S. National Paralympics Swimming team and we are rooting for you to go to Tokyo in 2021. How are you training while on campus?

LS: Easy. I swim from 6:00 to 7:10 a.m. At home I got up at 4:00 a.m. to practice before school.

Question: Can you tell us more about your swimming experience? Are you swimming at college?

LS: No, I signed up for the club team, but they aren't practicing right now. I want to swim on the varsity team, but there isn't enough space for me.

Question: Are you on a team or practicing on your own?

LS: Practicing on my own.

Question: What is that like for you?

LS: It's hard because I'm used to practicing with a coach every day.

Question: Do you wish it were different?

LS: Yes. I need to train so that I can make the team going to Tokyo next year. I want to go to Tokyo, and I want a medal.

Question: Do you have friends at college who swim?

LS: Yes.

Question: Are they on a team or just practicing on their own?

LS: Some are on a team, and some are practicing on their own.

Question: Do they practice with you?

LS: They don't practice with me. Because of coronavirus, it's only one person per lane, and we have to reserve lane times.

Question: What do you have to do to use the pool at UC?

LS: I go online and make appointments for lanes.

Question: How do you feel about this?

LS: It's okay.

Question: What are things that you think you need help with at UC?

LS: I want to know more about different classes. I am a little scared or nervous about work, so I focus on classes, work hard, focus on school.

Question: What are things that you don't need help with at UC?

LS: I keep a schedule, running laps, lifting weights. I eat breakfast, lunch, and dinner. I skateboard. I study and do homework, keeping on top. I focus on high grades. I just watch out and repeat what works.

Question: Have you met a lot of people since you've been at UC?

LS: Yes. It's all good. I have met people from all over Ohio and the world [by] playing football and swimming.

Question: How's the food on campus?

LS: Really good so far. I am on a meal plan. Overall, there is a wide selection of food like kabobs and yogurt. I don't want to lose weight.

Question: Why? Does this have to do with your training?

LS: I need to eat so that I don't cramp while I'm swimming. I don't want to burn muscle.

Note

Thanks go to Victoria Churchill for conducting this interview.

29

College Memories but Ready for What's Next

Amanda Pilkenton

My favorite memory from being a student at Georgia Tech is the time I met my class friends for the first time. When I came to school my freshman year, I met my two best friends, Maggie and Rachel, who are still my best friends today. I remember hanging out with Maggie and Rachel and going to different places around Atlanta with them. I also met other friends that are also in my year, and I have so much fun hanging out with my friends.

My favorite social clubs or organizations that I joined are the Excel sports committee, Omega Phi Alpha (a service sorority), and the LGBTQ community. I like being a part of the Excel sports committee because we plan small sports games, go to sporting events, and host intramural games. I love being a part of Omega Phi Alpha because we do service events for our school, community, and nation. I like meeting all the people that are a part of my service sorority. I am so happy I met the other members and to have been a part of the sorority. They are a good part of my college life. I also like being a part of the LGBTQ community because there are a lot of different types of people who join, and I have met different people there who I became good friends with. These friendships have taught me that I can be myself. It is great to have a community like this because you can learn about each other and about different experiences people go through. Also, you can just have another community you can talk to and relate to.

I have a couple favorite classes at Georgia Tech. Some of my favorite classes were Psychology and Biology of Sex and Death, which are classes that I took with all kinds of Georgia Tech students. Psychology is one of my favorite classes because I was always fascinated by the brain and how it works. I am also interested in biology because it is the makeup of the world around us and how it interacts with everything. Some of my favorite classes in the Excel Program were Health and Wellness and Social Diversity. They are my favorites because Health and Wellness teaches us how to keep us and our bodies healthy, and Social Diversity teaches us about the differences between different kinds of people around the world and how they interact with each other.

The most important thing I learned from college is to consistently manage my time because when I'm too busy, it can be difficult to do everything I need to do. I learned to manage my time by having a schedule for each day of the week. I use Google Calendar to keep track of all the tasks and events I have every day of the week. It is a good life skill to manage your time with all the things you do in life no matter how big or small they are. I feel like I will have a job that I love doing and be successful because I know how to manage my time.

Some advice I would give to my freshman self would be to not make my life more complicated by adding so much drama on top of work and classes. I say this because from the time when I was a freshman to around junior year, I had a lot of relationship issues between friends and dating relationships that caused drama, which affected my health and how I focused in school and at work. I went from very low moments in my relationships that I had, but I came back from those low moments by learning from them and the mistakes that I made. One example of when it was not working was when we had multiple arguments and didn't see the same things in the same way. I learned that in relationships people will have arguments and don't need to see things the same way as you do.

The advice I would give myself is to always focus on my studies and to never give up, no matter how hard it gets. Choose classes or topics you are interested in or want to pursue in life. Find clubs that you are interested in being a part of, and it is always good to make more friends along the way. It is good to have mentors and coaches to help keep you on track for socializing, academics, and just being there for you as a friend. It is good to rely on your coach and mentor when you need help with something.

What I learned from this is that I should always be persistent with the goals I am trying to accomplish and that I can't give up. I also learned from the beginning of college that often, you will have internships or jobs that you don't really like, but I have learned valuable things from these jobs, like how to be persistent even if a task gets difficult, being a good worker, and to work well with others. Not liking an internship job is okay because then you figure out what career you want to do, and then you can find jobs related to the career you want to do.

What I want in the future is to be happy and enjoy life. What I would want as a career is to be an assistant teacher to elementary school children. The subject I would love to help teach is science. Being at Georgia Tech has helped me decide this is the right job for me because I got to experience some internships that were related to education.

I would also like to have a good and steady, committed relationship. My experience in college has taught me how to have and keep that type of relationship going.

The hardest thing about the Excel Program is to schedule your time and to be organized and also to get your work done on time. Another hard thing is to find what career you want to be in. It might change over the years. Also, to find what kind of internship you really like and enjoy doing.

The best things about the Excel Program are meeting coaches and mentors and having best friends. Also, another good thing is having the experience of college life and joining clubs and organizations.

The people who impacted my life in the Excel Program are my

best friends, Maggie and Rachel, some of my coaches and mentors, my teachers in the Excel Program and outside, and also my Omega Phi Alpha sisters and student life community. They all have impacted my life in different ways. I could not get through college life without them.

The types of opportunities that I have in the Excel Program are being able to have a college experience, living on my own, doing my own chores, having coaches and mentors, meeting new friends, joining clubs and organizations, doing intramural sports, going to sports games, experiencing Georgia Tech classes, and having internship and jobs. I mainly get to have a great college experience and see what college is really like. I am so happy that I got the experience of being a college student with the Excel Program. I'm excited to graduate but not excited that I'm going to be out in the real world on my own. However, I feel ready because of everything I learned in the Excel Program.

30

Full Year of College

Luke Wilcox

My Scholars with Diverse Abilities Program (SDAP) experience was good. My friend Reid and I met Germaine, Robert, and Mara in our first year. We took Dr. Cummings's class in the morning, and my friends and I learned about independence and sex education. Before the class started, Dr. Cummings would do a meditation to help get our frustration out.

Back to sex education, one half of my brain said, "Luke, I'm out of here. I'm afraid someone might hurt you." But the other half of my brain said, "Luke, hold on, sex could help relieve muscle spasms. Believe me. Do you think that someone would hurt you? Um, yeah, no." I learned how sex can help to make babies. I learned what kind of love you have for a friend. Then the love gets a little stronger. Boyfriend and girlfriend alert. Holding hands. After that, it gets romantic. Buy something for them. I researched how to have sex in a wheelchair.

I went to Creative Writing in the morning with Addie, my friend and peer helper. I wrote stories and shared them with my classmates by hitting the speak button on my computer Tobii Dynavox, or TD for short. Mrs. Wineberger, my writing professor, had me and my classmates read WordPad prompts to write a story about everything each Tuesday and Thursday morning. Then we had to add fiction to our real stories a second time to get our imaginations to run wild. My classmates and I had to read short stories to get our writing even more creative, like how to describe what I am doing in my real story.

My friends and I took Beyond Normal in the afternoon, and I liked it. We summarized *One Amazing Thing*. My friends and I learned about disabilities. We had schoolwork to do, but we had Mary and Michael, my dear friends who are tutors, to help.

Then my friends and I talked about Coffee Talk. We cooked food on Thursday for the big day. At Coffee Talk, we had different roles on the second Friday of every month. I liked being a pep-talker because I gave my speech to my classmates. I said, "Hey everybody! It is Coffee Talk time. Remember class, don't forget to wash your hands before you serve the food. Remember class, don't eat the food. 1, 2, 3! Go Coffee Talk team! Woo-hoo!" After my speech, I was rolling all over the place at the College of Education building, trying to do my jobs like a chicken running around. Boy, I love it!

In my friends' and my second year, my friends and I met Clay, Nick, Daniel, Allen, Emma, and Elizabeth. We became friends with them. I will keep up with my friends, except for Germaine, Robert, Nick, and Daniel, because my friends don't keep up with me because they are too busy with their jobs or move away before school is out.

So, after I graduated from the Scholars with Diverse Abilities Program, I came back to Coffee Talk to see my friends. They were shocked. Clay said, "Hey, Luke!" I have good conversations with him. He always talked to me about girls. Back to Coffee Talk, first I didn't help like I did when I was at college. But I talked to new customers though.

Mary and Addie, my dear friends whom I'd like to call "sisters" because they act as sisters to me, and I went to the Appalachian State versus Coastal Carolina game on October 6, 2017. My "sisters" and I watched Appalachian State slaughter Coastal Carolina badly. I said, "Well, let's leave," in my brain. During the slaughter, Reid, Mara, Germaine, and Robert came by to see me. Mary fed me popcorn, then Addie fed me her ice cream because I was eyeing her ice cream. She said, "Here. You can have it. You are spoiled. Do you know that?" I laughed. After Appalachian State scored points in the fourth quarter, we left because we didn't want to see the game.

My friends and I took Dr. Cummings's class again. We learned about mailing and how to send mail to our parents when we are living far away. My friends wrote a letter to their parents, but I wrote a letter to my uncle and my aunt. I enjoyed it. My friends and I learned about alcohol. My brain said, "Um, I don't know about it."

I had some help to get my schoolwork done with Cori, a tutor whom I'd like to call "sister" because she acts like a sister to me, too. Boy, we got my schoolwork done before I went home. It was like . . . okay, here is schoolwork. Here is Cori. Here is me. Two on one handicap match. I fought my schoolwork, then I tagged Cori in. She fought my schoolwork for me, then Cori tagged me in. I put a final nail in the coffin on my schoolwork.

College was hard for me to move physically. Most of the people were doing this: separate, go around me, then come back together. The students didn't let me go, and I was frustrated. I said, "Can you move out of my way, please?" in my brain. But they let me go, and I said, "Thank you. Finally!" in my mind.

My classmates and I learned how to vote. It was cool because we voted for the first time. We learned about which candidates were doing right for the town of Boone, the state house, etc., to vote. My classmates and I did a presentation about which candidate will do the right thing for North Carolina, too.

My favorite classes were Interpersonal Communication and Intercultural Communication with Dr. Chris Patti. In Interpersonal Communication, I loved being in his class because my smile lit up the room. Then people started to smile. Dr. Patti told a story to the class, then I laughed. After I laughed, so did my classmates. Dr. Chris Patti told me, "Whatever you had on your mind, please tell us?" So, I told whatever I had in my mind.

In Intercultural Communication, Dr. Patti told me the same

thing. My classmates and I saw Mr. Patti's haircut. I was the first person to say, "Hey, Dr. Patti! Nice beard!" My classmates were shocked. Their facial expressions were like . . . Uh? Do you know him? Then Dr. Patti said, "Thank you, Luke!" to me. He told my classmates about me. They understood. We have been friends since then. I mean lifelong friends. We have continued to talk by email to each other ever since I graduated.

I met new friends at SDAP, and we talked during social time. After my friends and I graduated, we texted each other because I wanted to have lifelong friends, which became my friends forever after college. They are really close to me making them my family.

It was wonderful to go to college to learn and make lifelong friends with my tutors, my peer helper, and my professors.

31

My Favorite Memories in College

Elizabeth Droessler

I have worked at my farm since I was nine years old. I'm twenty-four, so I've been working on the farm a long time. On the farm, I feed the animals, like bunnies, guinea pigs, and birds. I also teach people to feed the animals and hold the animals. The guinea pigs like to be held more than the bunnies. During the day, I will put goat food for the goats in the pasture. I work at the farm at my mom's house.

I started the Scholars with Diverse Abilities Program (SDAP) in 2018 and graduated in 2020. While I was in SDAP, I did color guard, skiing, archery, and newspaper. I also really enjoyed photography and I took a lot of pictures. I like color guard because I did it for two years and in high school for eight seasons. In high school, I signed up and I went to practice. At Millbrook High School everyone was really nice, and I really enjoyed doing it. At Appalachian State, I liked color guard a lot better because college color guard was more fun and friendly. I made more connections with them when we went to New Orleans. I made new friends, and everyone was happier. I took pictures for the newspaper at App State. My mom also worked with the newspaper in 1983! For the newspaper, we had a lot of groups because we had a lot of people in the club. We would watch news videos. Also, during my time here, I did archery and skiing. For me, I started doing archery at home and then I did archery in college. In archery, your body is one line, and you have to face the target to shoot straight. This was my first time doing skiing, before Covid hit. I liked skiing, but I need to practice more. I had a hard time stopping so I want more practice.

One of my hobbies is photography. I was a teenager when I started taking photos. I saw my brother's camera and I started taking pictures. My brothers told me I had a really good eye for the camera. And now I love photography. I like to take pictures of animals and flowers, or anything really. I also took photos for Coffee Talk. Coffee Talk is where the SDAP students make breakfast and coffee and people can talk to the SDAP students about their lives. Coffee Talk is a happy time. I was able to take pictures of what was going on there. I got to take a photography class in the art building, and I loved that class. Once my friends knew I was taking photography, everyone wanted me to take their pictures. I also get to take pictures of the animals and the guests of the farm. I don't sell these pictures; I love to take these for fun and the guests love them too.

I got to travel with the school while I was a student. I went to NYC with my art class and to Washington, D.C., with SDAP. In NYC, I was in my art class, and we went to see plays and museums. My favorite plays that I saw were *Come from Away* and *Anastasia*. I also went to D.C. with SDAP. In D.C., we went to see museums and we explored the city. The museums were really cool, and I took pictures of what I saw. I took some pictures of the Holocaust Memorial Museum. My favorite picture was the one with all the faces. I really liked this art because I love to see different faces and their stories are interesting. It's sad too. Since I love photography, this piece was really interesting to me.

Now that I have graduated and moved back home, I am still taking a lot of pictures and am loving photography. I take pictures of animals and faces, or anything I can find. I have a job at the farm from ten to five and get to continue feeding the animals.

Part IV

Supporting Growth

PEER MENTORING AND SUPPORT

In this part, we see student authors as they offer suggestions to others as trailblazers in a reimagined space. These stories reflect the importance of allyship both among students and with others. We see here a reclamation of power as students are positioned, themselves, as the experts on their lived experiences.

These stories are critically important to our understandings of higher education. Why haven't these perspectives been acknowledged before? Why aren't these narratives recognized as part of the ordinary collective of college experience?

32

Communicating Successfully in College

Maia Chamberlain

For me, communicating takes extra time daily and a lot of extra steps to put the dialogue into my communication device for class presentations. The work is a little harder, but the rewards are worth it.

Using Sign Language vs. My Augmentative Communication Device

I communicate using sign language and an app on my iPad that speaks for me. Using sign language is my preferred mode of communication. It is easier for me to use, but people can't always know what I'm saying. I have known sign language since I was two years old. When I use my communication device everyone can understand me, but it is not always available or even quick enough for me to use. I think using my device to communicate makes people feel more comfortable because they know what I'm saying. They don't have to wonder how to talk with me. I've used some sort of augmentative communication since I was three years old. Either way, it is not always easy and takes a lot of time and hard work to have basic communication. It is important for me to always have more than one way to communicate, more partners to communicate with, communication strategies, and to know my communication environment. That helps me know when to use which form of communication.

Communicating in Class

In class I use both sign language and my device to ask and answer questions. When I'm home doing remote learning, I type in the chat box on Zoom or send emails with my questions. I know it is important to participate in class in college because I want to do my best in school. When doing projects for my classes, I can do Google Slides with videos embedded of me using my device to talk. Videos make it almost like I'm standing in front of class presenting. Other projects were shared by me completing them ahead of time and then sending them to my professor to help facilitate the sharing on Zoom. Another reason it is important to answer questions and comment in class is because it has helped other students get to know me. They would know that I use sign language, I'm nonverbal, and I'm smart. That helped them know me better and know how to talk with me. It leads to making connections and friends on campus. I am not shy. I will go up and talk to people. One day on campus, I noticed two classmates I had seen walking up ahead on their way to class. I ran up to say hi so we could walk together to class. Even though we had never talked before, they knew my name and how to communicate with me by asking yes/no questions until my aide could catch up to help interpret for me.

33

True Rafferty Interviewed

True Rafferty, with Nathan Heald

Editor's Note: This is a written transcript of an interview between True Rafferty and Nathan Heald. The audio version is uploaded to Manifold. We include the written version to increase accessibility.

Nathan Heald: Hello, this is Nathan Heald, and I'm here joined by True Rafferty. Hey, how's it going?

True Rafferty: Good. How are you, Nathan?

NH: Good. Well, again, my name is Nathan Heald. I'm a lecturer and career development coordinator with the Excel Program at Georgia Tech. And I'm here to talk with True Rafferty a little bit about his experience in the Excel Program. We actually started the program together four years ago when I started as a lecturer working with the Excel Program and True as a freshman. And we wanted to take some time to look back and think about some of the experiences True's had and what he's learned over these last four years. So True, I want to start out, just kind of tell me a little bit about yourself.

TR: Well, I'm a fourth year in the Excel Program now. And, when I when I first started, I felt a little bit of anxiety because, I mean, I didn't have any friends. And I was starting someplace someplace different and I felt a little bit lonely.

NH: Yeah. How's that changed? I think a lot of people go through that experience when they start college. They have an experience that they're not ready for, that they've never had before. How has that changed from your first year to your fourth year?

TR: Well, I've made some some new friends, but I've also done done some things to help push me out of my out of my shell a little bit.

NH: Okay, tell me about some of those things that you say "pushed you out of your shell."

TR: I joined some, I got involved in some activities here, here on campus, such as CCF.

NH: What is CCF?

TR: Christian Campus Fellowship.

NH: Okay, and what else are you involved with, and what other organizations do you get involved with on campus?

TR: Swimming club and outdoor recreation.

NH: All right. That sound like fun. And what are some of the activities that you did with those organizations?

TR: Well, for outdoor recreation, I went on a couple of sea kayaking trips. I wanted to do some caving, as well, but because of the pandemic, that didn't end up happening.

NH: Okay, what is sea kayaking?

TR: Well, that's where you take a kayak out on a out on a lake or the ocean and, you know, you just paddle like that, and instead of going down a river that's flowing. It's always moving. And the shape of the kayak is different than a white water kayak. A sea kayak has a more narrow body and a sharper nose.

NH: So you've learned a lot about different activities and sea kayaking is one of them. Do you think you're going to continue some of these activities after the Excel Program?

TR: Yeah. Yes, I do. I think I'm good. I think I'm going to continue to look for opportunities to to explore caves and also try other active outdoor activities as well.

NH: Okay, so you mentioned also CCF. Have you made friends there?

TR: I mean, I haven't made any friends but the people, the people there were really nice.

NH: Okay, do you feel like you've made friends over the four years in the Excel Program that you're going to continue afterwards?

TR: Yes, I think I'm going to continue to stay in touch with the friends that I've made here at Georgia Tech.

NH: How has that made you feel, knowing that you have friends that you'll stay in contact with after the Excel Program?

TR: It's made me feel like I've put myself out there and that feels great.

NH: Good, good. So we talked a little bit about social life and some of the activities you got to participate in. But another part of college is going to classes, right? Right. So what are some of the classes that you've taken? Maybe some that you really enjoyed since you've been in the Excel Program.

TR: One class that I thought it was pretty interesting was Abnormal Psychology.

NH: Okay, you remember anything you learned in that class?

TR: Well, just that the human mind is a very delicate thing.

NH: And I didn't mean to put you on the spot there, was that a class you took a few semesters ago?

TR: I took it last semester.

NH: Okay, what are some of the other classes you've taken that you've enjoyed?

TR: Sociology and supply chain management.

NH: Okay, very cool. So, how did you stay on top of all your classwork? So you have all these different classes that you took, but how did you manage to stay on top and stay organized?

TR: I prioritize my assignments by their due dates. So whatever was coming up soon. I got that done first and then whatever it was was due at a later time. I would focus on that next. But I also had tutors that helped me with some of my work and helped me keep on top of my my work.

NH: Okay. I think having people that help us reach our goals and stay on top of things is really helpful.

TR: Yes, it is.

NH: Tutors were really helpful in making sure you're keeping track of assignments. Good, so another big part of the Excel Program is jobs. So, internship and work experience. You take a career course every single semester when you're in the Excel Program. So, tell me a little bit about your experience with work and internships over the last four years.

TR: Well, I've gained I've gained a lot of work experience since I started in the Excel Program. I think my most most favorite internship experience was working at the Atlanta airport. I mean, while I was there, I worked as a wheelchair attendant and I helped people who had trouble walking, getting to where they needed to go.

NH: What are some of the skills you think you gained through that experience, that internship?

TR: I mean, customer service skills and also directional skills as well.

NH: Yeah, Atlanta is the busiest airport, and you had to figure out how to navigate that and get people at the gates they needed to get to.

TR: Right, right, right. Working at the busiest airport in the world. Yeah. And I managed to navigate it in just a short period of time.

NH: That's great. So tell me some of your other experiences, because you've had quite a few internships that helped you figure out things that you like to do and things that you don't like to do. What are some of those other experiences you had?

TR: Well, when I first started, I thought I wanted to work in forestry, but after a couple of trials, I mean I discovered that maybe it's not, that it's not for me.

NH: How did you get a trial in forestry? What was the internship that gave you that experience or gave you a glimpse into what it would be like?

TR: I worked with the Georgia Tech landscaping and I worked with an arborist. But it was a lot more complicated than I thought it would be. And having to wake up at, like, before the sun comes up, I mean, I just couldn't do that.

NH: Yeah. And you had to be out in the elements as well.

TR: Yeah, you know, no matter if it was if it was was sunny out or if it was raining or snowing. Yeah. We had to be out there, and I mean, and I, I just couldn't do that.

NH: I think a big part of internships is finding out things that we don't like to do so that we can find those things that we do want to do. That's part of the internship experience. And the college experience is figuring out what's a good fit for you. Great. So, True, tell me, what is something that you're most proud of during your four years in the Excel Program?

TR: I think what I'm most proud of is that when I leave here I'll be able to say that I've I've graduated college. I mean, like when I was younger, I didn't even picture myself going to college.

NH: Yeah. It's a pretty cool achievement that you can say you went to four years, you graduated, you had that experience, you learned about what you are interested in and what you want to do after you graduate, make friends that you have for hopefully a lifetime. Yeah, I think that's something really important to be proud of. So, as a fourth year, you've had lots of different experiences and probably gained a lot of wisdom through those experiences. What would you tell a freshman or somebody that's thinking about going to college for four years? What would you say to them? What advice would you give them?

TR: I would tell them to take initiative. And don't be afraid to try something different.

NH: All right, so any other advice that you'd give?

TR: I would say, I would also tell them to don't be afraid of not fitting in. I mean we now live in an age of acceptance. So, you know, put yourself out there, do something you were never able to do before.

NH: That's great. That's wonderful advice. So, True, thanks for spending some time with us, explaining a little bit about your experiences, the things you've enjoyed and that you'll take away from the Excel Program. Thanks for sharing your story with us.

TR: Yep. My pleasure, Nathan. All right. Bye.

34

College Program Experience

Gracie Carroll

My experience in the Scholars with Diverse Abilities Program (SDAP) was fun and I love it because you get to have peer support that shows you around the campus and where your classes are. When my schedule came out, I saw who my supports were, and I was nervous to meet them in person. For my class major and career exploration, I saw that my support was Sidney Branham. We started texting and met up on campus for class, and when I first met her, she was super sweet and we talked about ourselves and got to know each other. And now since that class is over, I have been texting and calling Sidney, and we are really good friends. We had lunch one day with my current support, Brenna, at the central dining hall. I introduced Sidney to Brenna, and they talked about their majors and other things.

My other class is yoga. Brenna is my support for that class. We do yoga on Mondays and Wednesdays. She is very nice and sweet, and she helps me with my assignments. Brenna was also my support for the hospitality house and the homeless shelter. She volunteers there with me every Tuesday and Thursdays from twelve to three. The workers there were super nice. I cooked for the homeless people, and I helped in the food pantry. My other support waited for me outside of the volunteer place. His name is Sunnit, and he was really nice. We talked the whole entire bus ride to the campus. We talked about what hall I am in and how my classes are going. My Beyond Normal class support is Joi Perry. She is so nice and helps me with assignments and group projects. She is helping me with my individual project on social work and disability. We meet every Tuesday and Thursday. My other class is sociology, and my support is Brenna. I have an academic coach helping me with the discussion in the sociology class. Her name is Mackenzie Mack, and she is very nice and helpful with my discussion. My supports are helpful because they have made my college experience better. I appreciate my supports because they help me with my assignments, and they are always willing to help me when I need it. When I am overwhelmed, they help me calm down so I can get my work done. I would not be as successful in college if I did not have their support. I really have enjoyed getting to know my supports and they are some of my greatest friends.

35

Teaching, Assisting, Reflecting

OUR EXPERIENCE WORKING TOGETHER

Phillandra Smith and Meghan Brozaitis

My name is Phillandra Smith, and I am a doctoral candidate (I'm sure I will be a candidate by the time this is published) in special education also pursuing a certificate of advanced study in disability studies at Syracuse University. For fun, I enjoy baking, gardening, and reading a good novel. A fun fact about me is that I am from the Bahamas, but I now live in Syracuse (the weather difference is definitely "fun"). Last semester, I was the instructor of record for the course Introduction to Inclusive Education and had the pleasure of working with an intern from the InclusiveU program, Meghan. Our class consisted of twenty-three students. The students were from diverse programs, including education, journalism, public relations, fine arts, and communications. This piece is a reflection that Meghan and I did using questions we created together at the end of the course. We thought of this reflection as a tool others could use to prepare for inclusive internships and as a way to reflect on our experience working together. I think we both walked away with points to consider and areas of improvement regarding our inclusive practices as a result of this reflection.

My name is Meghan Brozaitis, and I did my internship through InclusiveU. I was a teaching assistant for the course Introduction to Inclusive Education and I did other internships. I did office work and event planning; I was a peer trainer where I went to events with other InclusiveU students, like basketball games and Orange After Dark events. Orange After Dark are events on weekends. It's just an opportunity to meet other people. I was one of the peer trainers last year, where I took the InclusiveU students to bowling and we went to the New York State Fair and did all kinds of different events every weekend. I enjoy going for walks, and I like taking pictures of sunsets and nature. I like working with kids. One fun fact about myself is I am really good at taking pictures of sunsets. My role in the course this semester was that I helped out with the attendance sheets and with the activities that we were doing in the classroom, like drawing a circle for them to write in, and I talked to them about my experience of being a teacher.

Question: What did you learn about yourself from this experience?

Phillandra Smith: Tough question. I learned that I prefer teaching in person, mostly because I felt like a lot of our online sessions were boring. Although we got impressive course reviews (the best I've received since I started at Syracuse), I was not confident in my abilities once we shifted to teaching online. The move to online because of Covid-19 was rather abrupt. We had just enough time to figure out the technological aspects, but I don't think we had enough time to figure out engagement strategies. So, I guess I learned that I need to have some self-compassion and ask others for feedback before I beat myself up and start to feel like I've failed in epic ways.

Meghan Brozaitis: What I learned about myself from this experience is how to be a teaching assistant and how to work in a classroom, since I plan on working in classrooms.

Question: What were your responsibilities as an intern?

PS: Meghan was responsible for all things connected to attendance. She held on to attendance sheets and ensured students signed in. She also distributed whatever supplies we were working on that day. On the day I missed class, she ensured that the system was up and that the PowerPoint for the day loaded to the system. Meghan also graded extra-credit assignments. I think I should have pushed this a step further and asked her to give the students feedback on their extra-credit assignments.

MB: My responsibilities as an intern were doing the attendance sheets and helping out with the lesson plans for what we were going to do in class. The students emailed both of us when they would be absent so I could mark them as excused on the roster.

Question: Describe your favorite class session. What made that session great?

PS: My favorite class session was the one we did on tracking.[1] We started the session by looking at everyone's pets, and then Meg asked an opening question that got people talking even before I introduced the topic. Our students seemed happy, they laughed and shared, and Meg texted me after to say it was a good class. She hadn't done this before.

MB: My favorite class session was when we would do group discussion about getting to know each other like when you (Phillandra) called out if you have an iPod, an iPhone, what's your favorite color, and what made that session great was when everyone got involved.

Question: What is one activity you really enjoyed?

PS: There are two activities I enjoyed; one was our final reflection activity. Since we were all on stay-at-home orders, I asked the students to find something from around their space that represented their semester. One student brought dark chocolate and said her semester was bittersweet, another student brought his Crocs and said the semester had a lot of holes in it but he was able to "redesign" it to make it more pleasurable for him. I wish Meghan was given the heads-up to participate in this exercise. One thing I certainly regret was not having her added to the class Blackboard. Sometimes I would send announcements to the group about changes to readings or what they should expect in the upcoming session and then I would realize I didn't send this email to Meghan. I also enjoyed when Meghan assisted in preparing the gingerbread person on the poster for an activity. I remember her looking to me and I thought it was for guidance or approval. A student got up from their seat to encourage her about her drawing. It was a reminder that we are all learning and growing, and our lives and development are connected to others.

MB: One of the things that I really enjoyed was when I got to draw for one of the activities that the students were doing. They were writing in the drawing.

Question: Two things you wish you did more of . . .

PS: Requesting feedback after each session and/or sitting to discuss how the session went. After one class, Meghan texted me to say the class went well. I felt like that class went particularly well also, but I had not previously acknowledged how valuable her feedback would be and how we could troubleshoot ideas to improve. I didn't have to do any of this "alone."

MB: Talk more and do group discussion. I wanted to be more a part of what was going on when they were talking about it and seeing what they were talking about, and I just wanted to get to know them more, being more outgoing. I felt like I didn't talk much to the students.

Question: Three things you wish you had said . . .

PS: Thank you—I said it, but I could have said it more.

How would you like to engage with the students this week?

What ideas do you have?—More of this would be helpful to help Meg develop her skills as well.

MB: Good morning.

After they left, telling them have a nice day.

Getting to know them.

Question: Describe your least favorite class session. What didn't work in that session?

PS: I don't think I have one in particular, but whenever I felt like I was sitting there talking to folks and they wouldn't answer back, I felt horrible. I felt like I bored the students lifeless for a full eighty minutes.

MB: My least favorite class session was when we watched a movie. What didn't work in that session, and some of the students didn't pay attention and they were either on their phones or laptops.

Question: What topic was your favorite? Why?

PS: My favorite topic was tracking. The students seemed very engaged.

MB: My favorite topic was talking about the different disabilities and listening to what everyone had to say about it. This was my favorite because I have a disability, so it was interesting learning about it.

Question: Two points of growth over the semester? (What do you think you got better at?)

PS: I got better at being okay with things not being okay and just working with everything as is.

I got better at switching it up on the fly. Depending on the way class was going, things could be added or removed, and even though I spent all that time creating those Google Docs, the vibe of the class took priority.

MB: I think I got better this semester doing the attendance sheets and getting better at speaking in front of class.

Question: One thing that you would like your work partner to know . . .

PS: I want my partner to know that I am so grateful for her presence and all the work that she did this semester. I am a do-it-yourself person, and I struggle with asking for help. If you ever felt that I was not maximizing your full potential, it had nothing to do with you and a lot to do with me. I guess I was also concerned about how much work I could ask of you, since it was not a paid internship. But I want you to know that if I could, I would have paid you because you deserve it and more for all you brought to this course. Thank you for all you did and for your patience with me as we figured this out (especially once we moved to online).

MB: That it takes me time to get used to what I am doing at first, then I will get used to the job.

Question: What were you most afraid of during this internship?

PS: My greatest fear was that our students would not understand/grasp the unique value we both brought to the class. I stressed the need for us to connect theory to practice and since this was an inclusive education class, "presuming competence" was something we talked about at length, but I feared they would reserve what they learned for classroom contexts where they were the teacher/instructor and not settings like ours where they were the student. I feared that neither Meghan nor myself might meet their expectation for what competent should "look" like. Learning about inclusive practices and actively engaging in inclusive practices are two different things. To know is not enough, but the course content focused more on the "knowing" than "doing."

We wanted them to engage in inclusive practices in their daily lives, but the only attention given to the "doing" aspect would come through my personal reflections on the way they interacted with both of us (I acknowledge this is subjective). Since I have an awareness of the different ways Black people are constructed in the United States, I would always wonder what my students thought when they saw me, and I feared they leaned toward popular stereotypes and negative constructions. I have had students express in the past that they had never been taught by a Black person, so since this class was predominantly white, I was concerned. I've had the privilege of not having to think about this (being a Black educator) in my past since I am from a predominantly Black country; in some ways, I think my mind tries to make up for the lost time by overthinking about these issues. In addition, from the information the students shared with us, very few (less than 10 percent) of the students identified as having a disability, so I could only hope they put what we were teaching into practice and saw value in our unique existences.

MB: What was I most afraid of during this internship was that I didn't know what to expect at first, and I was nervous because I haven't been a teacher assistant before. Being a teacher assistant for the first time, I was afraid I was going mess up, like I was going to do something wrong—like when I talked in front of the class and handed out what they had to do in class.

Question: If we were to do this over, what are four things we would improve/do better in round two?

PS: I would increase the number of ways students were able to engage with Meghan. I would have ensured Meghan had more leadership roles that involved her being in front of or speaking to the students.

Plan the lessons together so that we planned for how she would engage.

Build our relationship before we started working together so we could set expectations for meaningful reflection.

Time was a limitation in most instances. As a graduate student, I didn't feel like I had a model for what this experience should look like. Most professors do not have interns; I had no reference point. I lacked an example of what this experience should look like for both of us. With a full course load and teaching, I felt like I was figuring some of this out as I went.

This is not to say I have never worked with interns; I have, but not in a university context and not in the United States. Culturally, I am not comfortable asking people to do things they are not paid to do. This meant that if Meghan had something else going on either before or after the class, I saw it as infringing on her personal time to ask her to assist in additional ways. In retrospect, I should have spent more time with her and the person coordinating her internship before we got started to get a sense of the goals they wanted to achieve. At least that way I would be able to provide her with tasks that assisted in the development of those goals while assisting me in some ways as well.

MB: Talking about what we are going to be talking about in class to each other before class, going over the PowerPoint and explaining it to me so I know what we are going to do, talking to each other a lot more, meeting after class and going over what we talked about in class. Well, what was hard about all of this is that I was busy—like with doing lunch after I got done with being a teaching assistant—so I didn't really have much time to go over the notes after class with Phillandra, and then I had belly dancing with my roommates, so I was involved in lot of activities on campus.

Question: What advice would you give to the person having your role next year?

PS: Make time to talk and build the relationship before the class starts. Ask about your intern's perceived strengths and weaknesses. Get ideas on how they want to be involved, and then try to challenge them to build on perceived weaknesses over the duration of the course. Make time to reflect, and remember, never ever be afraid to ask for help. Your intern has great ideas to share. Talk to the internship coordinator about the objectives of the internship so that you can provide a tailored, meaningful experience. I think if I did more of this, I would have engaged Meghan more. Instead, I had concerns about what I could ask of her, considering issues of confidentiality, and because she was not being paid for her service, I felt like I shouldn't provide too many tasks. As the person being paid, I felt like I should do the brunt of the work. This view neglects the possible skill building that could have taken place for Meghan if I had shared some of the tasks with her.

MB: When you first become a teacher, it is scary, and you don't really know what is going to happen, but be positive and keep a smile on your face and ask questions.

PS: This experience of working with Meghan has really made me reflect on my inclusive practice, not what I know or what I say, but also what I do and how I do it. How do I embody the practices I want my students to develop? Despite me teaching a course in inclusive education—a course I've been a part of for two years—when I reviewed this reflection months after we wrote it, I must confess to my feelings of embarrassment. I feel like I got a lot wrong; there is a lot I would have done differently. Nevertheless, I am grateful for the experience, and I hope someone can learn from the vulnerability of these reflections. Further, I am reminded that "inclusion" is not a final destination, not a final resting place that we arrive at. It would make me feel better if I could say and show that I was an expert on "inclusion," but I am not. Each day and each person bring a new opportunity for me to think about how I will engage with those around me. I think this piece can be helpful in reminding us that developing an inclusive mindset, along with inclusive practices, is a continuous process. Our goal should be to reflect on our encounters with each person we meet and the environments we meet them in and think about how we can best dismantle barriers that deny them opportunities to be successful—by whatever means they define *success*.

MB: I just got a new job at a day care, and I've been working there. I go into different rooms and help out in there. I am a break staff. I do their lunch breaks, and I think my internship taught me how to be confident in myself and ask questions. I do that at this job that I have now.

Note

1. Tracking is a strategy used in schools to separate students into groups based on their perceived academic ability. This happens for all subjects or certain classes and curriculum. Some schools may refer to this as streaming or phasing.

36

My Georgia Tech Excel Story

Maggie Guillaume

It all started on August 19, 2017, when I moved into my second home at Woodruff North Dorm at Georgia Tech in my freshman year. I was sad when my parents and boyfriend left, but I was ready to start a new chapter in my life. I had a roommate, and her name was Amanda. I remember the first week was busy because we had a whole week of orientation, which had a lot of fun activities. I was so happy that week because that's where Rachel, Amanda, and I became best friends. I thought it was so cool that Rachel is from New Jersey, which is a different state from Georgia! I went to my very first T-Night, which was at the Bobby Dodd Stadium; it was a lot of fun. Rachel, Amanda, and I even got a picture with Buzz, which made me so happy because it was the first time of us getting a picture with our mascot. The next day was my birthday. It was a good day because my parents and boyfriend came up and we went out to dinner to celebrate my nineteenth birthday! I went to my very first Georgia Tech football game with my coach Riley. I have joined the Catholic Center to meet new people and try to make some new friends. I met one of my good friends today, and her name is Taylor; she is a Georgia Tech alumnus now. I did go to some of the Bible studies to meet people. I also remembered when Riley and I decided to go to Amelie's French Bakery in December, and it started to snow so much! Then I had a whole month off for my winter break, which was a fast first semester of college.

The second semester started off fun because I went to a Georgia Tech basketball game with Amanda and Rachel, which was the McCamish Pavilion. While we were at the basketball game, we saw Buzz and asked him if we could have a picture with him, and of course we have a picture with him, which was a fun night. The following week, Amanda and I decided to go to another basketball game, and it was so much fun. I got my very first internship at Paper & Clay at the Student Center on the Georgia Tech campus. At Paper & Clay, I cleaned the paintbrushes and other materials. I also supported workshops with students while answering their questions. I provided arts and crafts materials needed by the students who were visiting the center. I also met our Excel Program mentor coordinator Emilee's puppy Oatmeal, which was the cutest! There was a fun event that the Student Center Programs Council planned to go to the Georgia Aquarium; that was where Amanda and I went to see all of the fishes and watch the dolphin show, which was really cool. I went to the Georgia State Capitol for the first time to go to the Inclusive Post-Secondary Education Advocacy Day, which was a good day because I did talk to my senator for like fifteen seconds. Toward the end of semester, we went to Warner's Broadcasting as a trip, and I really liked it because I learned more about the broadcasting career. I also liked seeing the NBA TNT room because that was where they would talk about the sports. That was the end of my freshman year!

My sophomore year started when I moved into the dorm on August 18th, 2018. Amanda was my roommate again. My parents and boyfriend came up again for my birthday, which was nice. One of my good friends and Berri took me to Jeni's Splendid Ice Creams for a late birthday treat, which was so nice of her to do that. I also explored more places off campus with my friends. I went to Ponce City Market, the BeltLine, and Caribou Coffee. Amanda's coach Selin invited Amanda, Bella, and I to a tea party with her sorority, which is Phi Mu. We had so much fun, and we got to dress up and wear our pretty dresses. Bella was a new freshman in Excel. I also got my second internship at the

Women's Resources Center in the Flag Building at Georgia Tech. At the Women's Resources Center, I have organized books in alphabetical order, inventoried materials, and helped out with crafts. It was a good internship. I really liked my supervisor and coworkers. I also did an Alpha Xi Delta Autism Speaks 5k with my coach Abby, my mentor Charlotte, and Amanda. It was a fun race. Two weeks later was homecoming, and my best friend Claire from high school stayed over that weekend and went to the game with me! We had a ton of fun, and we went to Marlow's Tavern together after the game. A few days after that, Rachel, Amanda, and I went to a Fall KATs and Dogs Party at Tau Kappa Epsilon to see all sorts of dogs. Rachel and I were so excited and happy because we both love dogs! I remember seeing a pug there, and it was so cute. Halloween is coming around the corner, and we had trunk or treating. That took place at the Georgia Tech Police Department. That was where we would go around some of the coaches' and mentors' cars and get candy from their car trunks. I call it the college version of Halloween. In November, my mentor at the time Emma, Rachel, Amanda, and I decided to take a nature walk around Piedmont Park to see all the fall leaves, and then after we got hot chocolate from (one of my favorite places) Caribou Coffee. The following weekend, my two of my friends from outside of Excel and George did an Autism Speaks 5k at Piedmont Park. It was sunny, and the weather felt great outside. I remember that George got into first or second place for men in our age group! He was so fast. That was a wrap for my first semester as a sophomore.

The second semester of my sophomore year started with me being really active. Amanda and I signed up to join a Zumba class at Georgia Tech Campus Recreation Center. It was so funny and embarrassing at the same time because it was the day where most of the fraternities were at their intramural basketball game. Just a week later, I did yoga for the first time with my friends at the Student Center. It was kind of hard, but I did it. During that week, I started my very first internship off campus. My internship was at

Children's Healthcare of Atlanta Scottish Rite in Sandy Springs, Georgia. The tasks that I had from working there were delivering gifts to patients' rooms, supervising the hospital gift shop and assisting visitors who came in, putting medical equipment on poles and delivering it to the Emergency Department, playing with patients to give them a positive experience, and assisting children who required robotic rehabilitation. That was a good and cool experience. I liked delivering the gifts to the patients' rooms to make them have a smile on their faces and make them happy and comfortable. My coach Natalia and I wanted to do a little shopping one weekend, and we went to Little Five Points in Atlanta, Georgia. It was such a cool area. We went into this thrift shop, and I bought a cute hat. We had so much fun! A few weeks went by, and Amanda and I decided to go to a fun event called Rock the CASA, where we listened to a lot of types of music and had dinner there. We had so much fun! They played the song "Let It Go" from *Frozen* and there were guys that were singing along to that song! I thought it was funny. A few days after that, Amanda and I went to a Georgia Tech baseball game, which was at the Russ Chandler Stadium. We both enjoy going to the baseball games because we both like watching baseball. The next big thing that happened was I got my first certificate in the Excel Program. I got my certificate for academic enrichment, social fluency, and career exploration. I was so happy about getting that. That was a wrap for my sophomore year!

My junior year started when I moved into the dorm on August 17th, 2019. The first week was fun because I got in touch with my good friend Laney, and we decided to get our nails done together on the first weekend back. That was her first time getting her nails done. My parents and older sister came up to celebrate my twenty-first birthday! I was always happy to see them coming up to have a birthday dinner with me. A few days after that, I started my second internship at the Frazer Center. I would have to say the Frazer Center has to be my second-favorite internship because it is getting close to the career that I want. The tasks that

I did at the Frazer Center were helping preschool students to prepare for nap time, making sure students wash their hands, wiping down tables after breakfast, and playing with the students during recess. I have joined a service sorority on campus, and it is called Omega Phi Alpha. I am so happy that I joined Omega Phi Alpha; all of the girls are so nice. My good friend Grace and I did a service project together, and it was called Capturing the Spirit Oakland at Historic Oakland Cemetery. We went on a spirit tour toward the end of the night of this project, and we had so much fun! A few days after was big/little reveal for Omega Phi Alpha. Our big/little is about we get a big sister in the sorority to help us if we need help and reach our hours goal. I was so excited to meet my big and family that I was in. It turns out that Rachel became my big sister! I was also a part of the Delta family. That was such a happy day! Then a few days after that was homecoming. Rachel and I went to the homecoming game. Georgia Tech was playing against the University of Pittsburgh. Then, the following week, Omega Phi Alpha had their semiformal, which was at the Bill Moore Student Success Center on campus. I invited my boyfriend to our semiformal, and we had a great time. I also had a great time seeing my beautiful sorority sisters in their pretty dresses. It was one of the best nights I ever had in a while. Just a week after was rose night, which was when I was officially in Omega Phi Alpha for sure! Then, a few days later, my boyfriend, another friend, Rachel, and I decided to take some fall pictures because it was such a great day and the leaves were so beautiful. They were red, orange, and yellow leaves. That was a wrap of the first semester of junior year.

The second semester started off with Rachel's birthday! She is finally twenty-one! I had so much fun celebrating with her, and we went to a restaurant called Barcelona Wine Bar in Atlanta, Georgia, for her birthday dinner! My spring internship took place at the Howard School. My tasks at the Howard School were signing in students as soon as they entered the classroom, assisting students with opening their juice boxes, putting up and stacking down chairs, and using walkie-talkies to verify and record students' departure times. A few weeks after that, Omega Phi Alpha had recruitment week. Our theme was NU Bids on the Block. At the end of January, there was a little farm on campus, and I was so happy because I saw a goat! I love goats because they are so cute! Amanda got a bid in Omega Phi Alpha. I was so happy for her to join Omega Phi Alpha. A few weeks later, Amanda and I went to a Georgia Tech basketball game! We ended up getting a free shirt from that game! I actually liked my shirt because it said "Tech Basketball" on it! A few weeks after that game, my teacher Ashley and I went to my high school, the Cottage School, which is in Roswell, Georgia. We went there for a college fair to talk about the Excel Program. I was so happy to go back to the Cottage School to talk about the Excel Program. The following week, we went to the Georgia State Capitol for Inclusive Post-Secondary Education's Advocacy Day. It was a long day, and I was sad because I didn't get to talk to my senator that day, but I saw some of my friends that were in the Kennesaw State University Inclusive Program. A few days after that, I did a service project with Omega Phi Alpha and it was at the Reece Center in Palmetto, Georgia. The Reece Center was where we helped students with learning disabilities on their therapy riding horses for the Mental Health Project. A few weeks later we had a big/little reveal again. I actually signed up to become a big in Omega Phi Alpha because I wanted to be good friends with my little. When it was time, I got my little, and her name was Madeleine. She is a regular sophomore at Georgia Tech. As soon as she joined our Delta family, we were getting bigger because last semester we didn't have that many people. I was receiving a little sister in our sorority. I love my Delta family. The following week was spring break, and then we all got an email about all of our classes being pushed onto online due to a virus called Coronavirus. Everyone had to stay home after spring break and could not go back to college for the rest of the semester. We had to do our classes virtually for the rest of the semester. Then, one weekend my dad and I had to go back on campus to get all of my things. That was a wrap of my junior year.

My senior year hits off differently this year. I started class on August 17th, 2020, virtual edition. It was an interesting first day of school because I was at home this year instead of being on campus. At least I got to start my internship during the first week. This semester I am interning at the Cottage School in Roswell, Georgia. I am honestly so happy to have this amazing opportunity to intern at the best school. The Cottage School is one of the internships that I always wanted to try to get to intern at and happily I get to. At the Cottage School my tasks are assisting students with various activities based on classroom and student needs, monitoring and correcting classroom behavior, distributing classroom materials and handouts, using administrative equipment to prepare classroom materials, and registering all homeroom classrooms for sports or afterschool participation. I would say interning at the Cottage School has to be my favorite internship so far because it is relating to the career path that I want, which is to become a teacher assistant. The following week was when we had a virtual Omega Phi Alpha Coffee Chat for our fall recruitment. I am so happy to be still involved with Omega Phi Alpha, even though I am doing it from home this semester. Then I was happy to finally celebrate my birthday at home with my family and boyfriend this year. Recently, I got to meet my coach Emily for the first time instead of the computer screen. We went to get coffee from a place close to my internship site, which is called Crazy Love Coffee House in Roswell, Georgia. Then we went to Target. I had so much fun with her. Hopefully, we will do that again over winter break and have my other mentor, Mia, to join us as well. I am so excited to see what other things will happen to me this and next semester.

37

Emma's Journey

Emma Miller

Hi, my name is Emma, and I graduated from the Scholars with Diverse Abilities Program (SDAP) at Appalachian State University. I love to play piano. I taught myself how to play the piano when I was two years old. My favorite singer that I love to listen to is Taylor Swift. I saw her in concert five years ago.

I'm legally blind. I was born prematurely. I was born in July and was supposed to be born in November. It was very hard for my family because I was born so early, and I had to stay in the NICU for four months after I was born. I've been able to do a lot of things by myself that I didn't know that I could do. When I had the opportunity to go to college, I learned how to do things independently.

I was a part of SDAP at App State for two years. SDAP is the Scholars with Diverse Abilities Program. It's a two-year program with people who have all sorts of different disabilities. I was able to live in a dorm. The things that I learned how to do independently are doing my own laundry, making my bed, navigating campus, being on a schedule, and making sure to wake up on time for my classes every day. I also advocated for myself and my needs, learned how to vote, learned how to make pancakes for Coffee Talk, cleaned the bathroom, and learned how to ride the bus. I also made it on time to my work shifts at the dining hall.

While at App State, there were a lot of classes that I enjoyed taking. The three classes that I really enjoyed were Gerontology, Music Therapy, and College and Beyond. In Gerontology class, we learned all about aging. I really enjoy working with older adults, so this class helped me learn more about all the different aspects of aging and how it affects someone. Throughout this class, I was able to learn more about older adults that I didn't know before. The other class that I enjoyed was Music Therapy. In Music Therapy, we learned about using music as a form of therapy for older adults. This was an exciting class that I enjoyed so much because music and older adults definitely have a special place in my heart. College and Beyond is a class where we had lots of different goals and learned how to do things independently. We had four different types of goals. These goals were career, social, academic, and personal independence. These goals were helping me stay on track every week.

Working at the dining hall on campus, I helped serve customers by asking them if they wanted any side dishes to go with their entrées. I loved doing that because I love socializing with people. I'm very social. I also did an internship at a nursing home in Boone called Brian Estates. I love working with older adults very much. Older adults definitely have a special place in my heart. I played lots of different songs on the piano for the residents. I tried to play pieces that they would recognize. I had dinner with them a lot and had conversations with them to get to know them. I have so much experience working with older adults in assisted living. I started working when I was a sophomore in high school. I help out with all sorts of activities at the nursing home in Raleigh that I currently volunteer at called the Cypress Retirement Home. I play chair volleyball, call out bingo, help out with bowling, play the piano and sing for the residents, and watch cooking demonstrations.

While I was at App State, I was a part of lots of different clubs. I did Young Life, which is kind of like church. I've been a part of Young Life since high school. I wanted to make sure to continue it while in college. What we did at Young Life was play games, sing karaoke, do trivia, and made prayer requests if anyone had any, and we prayed.

I was in an a cappella group at App State called App Chorale. We sang lots of different songs, and I had two supports with me. Their names were Kallie and Ali. It was so great having them help me out with my music whenever I needed help. They really enjoyed the singing and being there with everyone. I also helped out with an event called Coffee Talk once a month. Coffee Talk is an event with SDAP where the students make and serve breakfast and coffee for whomever would come in the morning. We would also socialize with whomever comes. I did a lot of things at Coffee Talk: I helped set up the tables and chairs, I collected money from people, I made bagels, I served customers, I made coffee at Beans to Brew, I helped close Coffee Talk at 10:45 when it ended, I helped take everything down. I made my favorite thing, pancakes. I enjoyed making pancakes so much because pancakes are one of my favorite things to eat for breakfast and in general. I loved serving pancakes to customers. Making pancakes always puts a big smile on my face.

Overall, my college experience at App State was amazing. At first it was a little scary. Moving away from home and being three hours away was so scary at first. I was missing home and missing my parents so much. They didn't like me being so far away from them because they were worried about me and wanted to make sure that I was safe. Once I was there and after I adjusted, I got comfortable with my roommates and met a lot of new people. I went from the most concerned student to the most proud and independent student. I graduated from SDAP in the spring of May 2020.

38

Come Read about My Awesome Journeys through Life

Brianna Silva

Hi, my name is Brianna Silva; I am nineteen years old and I am from Wilmington, North Carolina. I am currently a freshman at Appalachian State University. I have a learning disability when it comes to reading, writing, and math; I am just like a normal human just struggling with certain things. Growing up, I really didn't know what I had; I could do everything. Whenever my teachers would start having parent-teacher conferences, my teachers would bring up to my mom that I might have a learning disability. That is when it was decided to put me in another class to see if the extra help was what I needed to be successful. But when it came to school, that's when it started to hit me that I might need more help. Around first or second grade, they started having me go to a separate class to help me with the subjects that I struggled with; this happened all through elementary school once they saw I needed help. When I made it to middle school, I would always have two normal classes and then two separate classes that would help me as well. Going into high school, I would have English, math, science, and an elective class; some of my classes would be a lot different from regular classes. The classes would be smaller and less hard so that the teachers could really take the time with each student so that we could be successful. When it came to quizzes and tests in the classroom, I would usually step out because I would need a modified test. My college experience is going pretty well, and I met some really great people already. My classes have been going pretty well, all things considered, all online, which is kind of hard sometimes. I like how in the Scholars with Diverse Abilities Program (SDAP) they have assistant supports that help you with your schoolwork, etc. I have explored some areas in Boone, and I am trying to find more places to explore with my friends. I want to let people know that if they have a child or know someone with a child that has some kind of disability and if they are looking for some colleges to make sure their child is getting the right help in college, in my thoughts I think they should come and visit Appalachian State University because they have a really great program and they will make you feel loved and cared for.

From my personal point of view, I was always accepted, I was never left out of things. Everyone saw me for who I am and not my disability and that made me happy inside because they treated me like any other high school student. My advice to whoever feels left out of things or who is different from others is don't let that affect you and the person you truly are and that you are never alone because everyone is different and nobody is perfect.

39

My Social Experience throughout Georgia Tech

Rachel Gomez

I remember coming to college as a nervous freshman and being super worried about how to make friends. I was worried that I would not have a lot of friends. But on the first day of freshman year, I met Maggie and Amanda. Ever since then, they have been my closest friends, and I know that I will always have them.

I am a Jewish girl from the suburbs of New Jersey, so I decide to join Chabad. Chabad is a home away from home. I have gone every Friday night for shabbat ever since my freshman year. Shabbat is a great way to spend time with friends, it is a great way to de-stress from your schoolwork, and you get to eat amazing food. Chabad will always be welcoming, even when I graduate. I also go there for the different Jewish holidays. There are a lot of nice people that attend there; not just Georgia Tech students but also Georgia State students go to Chabad. I met this really nice girl named Shani who went to Georgia State but transferred to Georgia Tech and is engaged to her boyfriend, Ethan. She is so nice, and we hang out and talk at shabbat and she offered me a ride home one time. She and her fiancé helped me get through my breakup with my ex-boyfriend. She told me not to worry, and we are now Facebook friends! I met a nice boy named Jacob last year at Chabad who goes to Tech. We talk and sit together at Chabad; we even walk home from Chabad together, and we follow each other on Instagram. I hope I can still see them at Chabad after I graduate. I hope I can stay in Atlanta so I can continue to see them at Chabad every Friday night.

Chabad is not the only source where I find my friends. Another place I found my friends has been through Omega Phi Alpha (OPA). Omega Phi Alpha is Georgia Tech's only service sorority. I was the first Excel student to join a sorority, and I eventually got three of my friends to join after I did! I always wanted to be part of Greek life and to join sisterhood and make lifelong friends. I pledged my first semester sophomore year, but I did not get in because I was too focused on my guy friends and on my ex-boyfriend. After I ended it with my ex, I was able to focus and become active in Omega Phi Alpha. My junior year was my first active semester. It was hard to get all my service hours because I was sick. I almost got kicked out because I had a hard time getting all my service hours, but they were so understanding. OPA has been a great experience for me, and same with Chabad, because it made me get out of my comfort zone. I am proud of my leadership by being the first Excel student to join a sorority. I made such an impact in Excel that my two best friends, Maggie and Amanda, joined Omega Phi Alpha. Maggie joined her first semester of her junior year; I am Maggie's big sister in Omega Phi Alpha. My second friend, Amanda, joined her second semester of her junior year. I also got a new friend in Excel to join Omega Phi Alpha; she is a freshman, and her name is Lily. I am also friends with the other girls in it but would love to do more things with them. I would also love to do more things with Maggie and Amanda or just the other girls in the sorority. We do a lot of fun in-person service activities. One service project that is super fun is going to the Reece Center, which is helping children and young adults with autism and Down syndrome to ride horses. That is my favorite service project because I used to ride horses when I was little.

I had a lot of great experiences over my four years of Excel. I love Georgia Tech and I would have never wanted to go to a different college! College has been great for me because in high school

I did not have a lot of friends or a group of friends. I was afraid college would be the same as high school, but it has been different and wonderful; I have more friends now than I ever did! Chabad and Omega Phi Alpha were really great experiences. I am glad I was able to join a sorority and continue my religion. I am glad that I got out of my comfort zone to join a sorority and to branch out at Chabad. My advice for incoming freshman would be to not be shy and to try different clubs and organizations. If you liked volunteering in high school, then try to find a volunteer option in college; you can find a group of friends that way also. I think these can be lifelong friends that I met through OPA and Chabad. I know that I will always have Maggie, Amanda, and Lily as friends.

40

The Importance of Goals

Tyler Shore

My name is Tyler Shore! I am a second year in a two-year program called the Scholars with Diverse Abilities Program (SDAP). My favorite thing that I like to do in SDAP is work on goals. The goals that I work on in SDAP have four categories. The categories are social, career, academic, and personal.

Personal Goals: The personal goal that I have currently is how to track when I am stressed. Other personal goals I have had in the past were doing yoga poses; riding the AppalCART, which is a free bus system that runs throughout Boone, by myself; forming healthy habits (e.g., drinking water); being flexible when there are changes in my schedule; and creating a budget/spending plan for shopping.

Social Goals: The social goal that I have currently is getting to know more people. Other social goals I have had in the past were being with Best Buddies, engaging in clubs (e.g., App Chorale), hanging out with people that were in clubs with me as well as other people (e.g., my peer support group for my Beyond Normal class with Rebekah Cummings that I took my first year in SDAP). I have also gone to Awesome Squad, talked with friends through FaceTime, and researched the radio station club.

Career Goals: The career goal that I have currently is studying libraries. Other career goals that I have had in the past were being a radio DJ, training at different jobs at the library, being a librarian, and working on library stuff from home (e.g., looking for dead links on the library's website).

Academic Goals: The academic goal that I currently have is researching libraries. Other academic goals that I have had in the past were researching music, learning about autism (my disability), working in the workbook *Autism: What Does It Mean to Me?* by Catherine Faherty, thinking of specific music and drama classes I would like to take, being a strong student and completing assignments, and doing an assignment called "Common Reading Homework."

Common Reading Book: The common reading book I read was called *Just Mercy*. It is about court cases (e.g., the Walter McMillian case). That assignment was for my Beyond Normal class. I also had to attend a talk from the author of that book at the Appalachian State University Convocation Center (where my high school graduation was and where my college graduation will be). His name is Bryan Stevenson. My favorite part of the book was when Walter McMillian went to Montgomery, Alabama.

Work/Internship Goals: The work/internship goals and skills that I have at Belk Library are collecting, strengthening, and picking up library materials, arranging library materials on book carts or in reshelving areas, responding to requests (customer service), putting books and DVDs in the right order, learning how to take direction from my supervisor Kyle McFarland, communication, independent navigation, using the Library of Congress classification system (nothing comes before something), and filling out my timesheet. "Nothing comes before something" is a saying that helps remind me how to place library books in the correct order. The work/internship goals and skills that I have in Literacy-Cast (online in Zoom and also an internship where people read books and are teachers in the program) are working with reading clinic assistants (e.g., Devery Ward or Beth Frye) to plan and prepare for Literacy-Cast sessions with K–12 students, reading to the K–12 students, sharing stories from my life experiences during Literacy-Cast, communicating with others, planning with partners, reading, advocating, and leadership. The work/internship goals that I have at WASU (radio station at Appalachian State University, also called the Beasley Media Complex) are following directions for what is given during my hour at WASU, communicating with WASU staff, using hand sanitizer to clean my hands before touching the equipment, cleaning the equipment after using it, bringing and using headphones, bringing and using a windscreen, communicating with others, and radio station operations. I also did an internship at Beans 2 Brew (a coffee shop on App State's campus) the first half of spring 2020. My goals and skills for that job were telling customers to donate purchases through SDAP, making it to scheduled shifts on time, preparing and serving orders to customers, performing multiple tasks at the same time, communicating clearly, and adhering to proper food-handling techniques. My favorite job to work at is Belk Library because I like to shelve books. Internships are important because they help you to prepare for getting a real job later in life.

Supports I Have Had: I worked on WASU stuff with my support for my Mass Communication class. I have had three person-centered planning (PCP) advisers as of now. PCP advisers are also called graduate assistants. I did the PCP meetings in person at the College of Education building and online in Zoom. I have also had other supports for different classes. They are called in-class supports. I also have college life fellows helping me in the dorms. I also had three supports who went to Washington, D.C., with me and my SDAP friends. These supports helped me with homework and classwork for different classes that they supported me in. Supports are helpful because they can show you where classes take place and help you do a good job in classes.

Classes That Are Helping Me with My Goals: College and Beyond class helps me with my personal, social, career, and academic goals. Career and Practical Living helps me with my work/internship goals. I have also taken classes that have helped me with my communication goals. A couple of them are Public Speaking and Mass Communication.

Coffee Talk: The building that Coffee Talk was in was also the College of Education building. I also did Coffee Talk when I was in fifth and sixth grade at Hardin Park School and freshman through senior years at Watauga High School. Coffee Talk is an event that happens once a month on Fridays. We get to make breakfast items like cheesy eggs and hash brown casserole. My favorite thing about Coffee Talk is serving people their food.

My D.C. Trip with SDAP: I went to D.C. with SDAP last year. The Multicultural Department led the trip. The leaders were Kendall Rankin and Jerisha Farrer. I toured different museums like the Mexican Cultural Institute, the Holocaust Memorial Museum, and the American History Museum. I also got to spend time with my aunt JoEllen Carpenter and my uncle Mike Carpenter while I was there. I got to stay in a hotel called Courtyard by Marriott. My roommates in the hotel were two guys named Redeate Sisay and Sequan Patterson. I mostly learned about historic people like Adolf Hitler. This trip was important because we also got to learn about different cultures.

Awesome Squad: Awesome Squad was an event where people met twice a month on Fridays. It was at the Wesley Foundation. We would mostly watch movies, have snacks, and play cornhole during those events.

My SDAP Friends: I have a lot of friends that are in SDAP with me. Their names are Makayla Adkins, Taylor Ruppe, Micah Gray, Grace Carroll, and Bri Silva. When I first started SDAP, there was Emma Miller, Clay Medlock, Allen Thomas, Elizabeth Droessler, Daniel Rudasill, and Keiron Dyck.

I am so excited for my future after SDAP moving forward. SDAP has really helped me with getting through college life and life after college. I hope to live in an apartment in Boone, North Carolina, and work at the Watauga County Public Library in the future. My favorite things that I did at that library when I was a volunteer there were shelving DVDs and cleaning books. The apartment I hope to live in is through a nonprofit called LIFE Village. It is where adults with disabilities live. I also hope to do more radio DJ stuff as a hobby.

41

Support and Encouragement for the Ones Who Seek It

Elliott Smith

Edward Ridge felt important as he moved into his apartment for college. He had the dream to become a teacher's assistant, and he knew that his college program for young adults with disabilities would have that become a reality. Another young girl, named Alice, was also moving into the same building to be in the same program, and so was a young boy named Andy, who was hoping to become a chef. After the first semester ended and the second one began, Andy started an internship at a Greek house on campus, which was not super busy. He loved that a lot. Edward started working at the Frazer Center, while Alice started working at the Elaine Clark Center because she also wanted to be a teacher's assistant. Both the Frazer Center and the Elaine Clark Center are private schools for preschool through high school. One day, Edward and Alice met up to go out for fun with some friends. As they waited for some friends to show up, they talked about what classes they were in.

"I'm taking a history class now," said Edward. "It's Civil War to Present."

"I'm taking a history class, too!" said Alice. "Except it's all American history."

"You love history?" asked Edward.

"I do," replied Alice.

This conversation went on until the group of friends left. Later, after summer at the start of a new year, Andy got a job at the campus food court. He liked this chef work, but the food court sometimes got too busy, and Andy wasn't a fast cook. Some of the equipment was heavy, and customers and coworkers sometimes complained and acted weird. Andy often came back to his apartment grumpy and short-tempered. He didn't feel like hanging out with friends on weekends, and when he had activities planned, he wanted them to go exactly the way he expected them to go.

"I don't know what's gotten into you, Andy!" Edward said one day. "It's clear to me that you need to find a different job at a place that's less busy or easier."

"Like where?" asked Andy.

"Like the ice cream shop that my dad started," suggested Edward.

"Your dad started an ice cream shop?" asked Andy. "You didn't tell me that!"

"There aren't many locations around yet because the company is still expanding," Edward said. "The place still gets crowded on hot days, but all you'll be making is ice cream, milkshakes, or frozen yogurt, and that's all."

"What's the name of the place?" asked Andy.

"Glen and Ridge Ice Cream House," answered Edward.

One week later, Edward was walking through the lobby of his apartment building after coming back from a class when he saw Alice sitting on a couch crying. He sat across from her.

"What's wrong, Alice?" asked Edward.

"I was out to dinner at Marlow's Tavern, and we were supposed to pay separately, but the server didn't listen, and I paid for all the dinners, as well as my own," sobbed Alice.

"I'm sure it was only an accident," said Edward.

"All of my friends said that, but my parents didn't think so," said Alice.

Edward gave Alice a hug and gave her a tissue to dry her tears.

When he got back to his apartment, Edward started thinking about times when he talked to some girls and thought about dating them. Some of the girls he thought of, though, had hard times talking and others acted funny.

"I would've regretted asking any of them out," he thought.

Suddenly, Edward got an idea. Later that weekend he called Alice.

"Would you like to go to dinner with me?" Edward asked.

"I would love that!" answered Alice. "I'm free tomorrow for dinner."

"So am I!" answered Edward. "I'll see you tomorrow!"

The next day at 6:00, Edward met Alice in the lobby. She was dressed in a beautiful dress covered with flowers of spring.

"You look so pretty," said Edward.

"Thank you," said Alice.

The two walked down together to Moe's Southwest Grill, where they got their favorite Mexican dishes. When Edward and Alice began talking, they soon realized they had a lot in common. At the end of the dinner, Alice thanked Edward for paying and the two went back to their apartments. Next week, Alice met Edward on the twenty-fifth floor to talk, and they found even more common interests. They both loved kids and their jobs as teachers' assistants that they planned to keep for years.

"I work with about twenty preschool kids at the Frazer Center, and I love it," said Edward. "What about your job?"

"I work with eight- and nine-year-olds at the Elaine Clark Center, and they all have disabilities," Alice told Edward. "I also want to know how you get there. I use the MARTA trains. I ride it to Chamblee."

"I use MARTA to get to the Frazer Center as well," replied Edward. "Except I ride a bus."

"I've never used a MARTA bus before," said Alice.

"It's easy to do it when you know where you're going," said Edward. "But if you're more comfortable using the trains, we can do that someday; maybe ride up to the mall and shop."

More and more common interests were found as the conversations went on for Alice and Edward. They started going on more dinner dates every week. Later, Andy got an interview for a job at Glen and Ridge Ice Cream House and got the job. The shop was busy, but he loved making ice cream and frozen yogurt much better than meat and salad, which was what he used to do at the campus food court. Edward and Alice went on dating and gave gifts to each other whenever they felt like it. Soon, they had met each other's families, who were very happy to see these two together. After working for two years at Glen and Ridge Ice Cream House, the company expanded and opened up more locations, and Andy became the manager of his store after Edward's dad retired. After Edward, Alice, and Andy graduated from college, Edward wished to find a way to share with everyone how awesome it had been giving support and encouragement to other students, and that is exactly what you have now finished reading.

The end.

Coda

Why This Collection?

Beth Myers and Michael Gill

This project started five years ago over a chance interaction at a writing retreat for junior faculty in our school. Both of us were working on other projects. Separately, we had been considering how to best facilitate and curate sharing of student experience in inclusive higher education. We began to think about this project in new ways, considering our students and all students as publishable authors with truths that needed telling. From the beginning, we believed that whatever was put together would begin to shift the landscape and discourse around inclusive higher education. We could never have imagined the collection that did emerge.

We have our own complicated histories with higher education. Michael enrolled in four separate undergraduate institutions. Along the way, he lost transfer credit and the wish of finding a perfect, welcoming campus experience. He worked full time throughout a majority of undergrad (and graduate school) and only lived on campus for the first semester of his first year. When looking for academic jobs, a professor cautioned Michael to take off his community college experience from his CV, thinking it would jeopardize his job prospects. (He didn't take this advice. He is a proud graduate of Spokane Falls Community College.) With each passing year of college and academic job rejection, he learned how it supposedly mattered where you went to college and what your pedigree was. Of course, it doesn't have to be this way, but academia and academics often reinforce the same ableist, racist, classist, and exclusionary models they (sometimes) critique.

Beth had a more traditional undergraduate experience, with four residential years at a small liberal arts college. Now in academia, she is realizing that it was her graduate student experience that was not the norm for a future university professor at a research institution. She took all of her doctoral courses part time while teaching students with disabilities full time in an inclusive elementary school, the first years of inclusion for autistic students there. She concentrated not on research and publication but on the practice of inclusion on a daily basis. Beth then took a meandering path to becoming an academic, pausing her doctoral work multiple times. She completed her coursework, moved states, opened a disability-focused nonprofit, had a baby, completed her comprehensive exams from afar, had another baby, proposed her research, ran the nonprofit center, had another baby, and finally completed her dissertation. This circuitous road took six years longer than she had planned, and she eventually ended up with four children and a (initially non-tenure-track) position at a university. We all struggle with the ideas imposed by others about who belongs in higher education and who does not.

Disabled advocate Judy Heumann famously said, "Independent living is not doing things by yourself. It is being in control of how things are done."[1] Likewise, professor George Dei reminds us, "Inclusion is not bringing people into what already exists; it is making a new space, a better space, for everyone."[2] These ideas are echoed throughout this collection in an emergence of agency as students share their experiences of inclusive higher education. Kailin Kelderman, Eilish Kelderman, and Mary Bryant's piece "Being Independent Has Risks" confronts issues of safety and the dignity of risk for people with intellectual disability. We learn, in that piece, how Kailin renegotiated control over her own future despite a terrible wrong. She and her family were able to balance the seemingly competing desires of safety and agency. Antonio E.

Contreras also demonstrates his self-determination in the first student chapter, "I Want to Go to College"—through his persistence from one college to the next, moving away from his parents both literally and figuratively, and in expressing his goals for his future. This self-determination does not grow in a vacuum; students gain access to skills and knowledge in higher education that support this growth, just like other college students. Antonio, Kailin, and many other student authors have incredible communities of support that have enabled their journeys and choices. Some parents of individuals with intellectual disabilities continue to be the best allies in challenging ableist systems that consider intelligence to be fixed. In the essays, some authors remark how parents were able to assist the search for college or even help move them across state lines. We know that not all students have this type of parental and family support. Admission to college should not be dependent upon social mobility or parental interest and resources. In our own program, we know the importance of engaging with students and their communities early in the high school experience to help facilitate access to higher education for students who did not previously imagine it could be a possibility. As administrators and educators, we need to continue this vitally important work, especially as opportunity expands in campuses, to ensure our programs are not just for those from upper- and middle-class white families.

We also wanted to examine ideas around receiving support and to reconsider how we think about grit and meritocracy in higher education. In "Taking the Llama for a Walk and Other Things That Helped Us," Olivia Baist and Kylie Walter show us that the complex relationship of friendship and support does not negate the college experience but enriches it. Yet, we are also aware of how this type of support is not without struggle, as Olivia and Kylie discuss. If readers have not watched their documentary (*And They Were Roommates: Navigating Inclusive Mentorship in Higher Education,* linked to on the Manifold site), we encourage you to. The film expands upon their chapter, highlighting the complex ways that both needed support from each other and their communities. In "Teaching, Assisting, Reflecting: Our Experience Working Together," Phillandra Smith and Meghan Brozaitis address issues of presumption and belonging. Both came to the classroom with their own notions of outsider identities and navigated the expectations of higher education. Kieron Dyck, in "Inclusive College for All and How My Perception of My History Prof Changed," writes about how he worked with his history professor to seek the accommodations needed to succeed in class. Many discussed how online learning during the pandemic was challenging. The students sought community and wanted to thrive by receiving in-person support and encouragement. Inclusive higher education challenges traditional ideas about meritocracy and who belongs in college. Can one still be a successful college student if they receive support? If their classes are modified? If they access the university in an alternative way? These programs and students push us to rethink inclusion and postsecondary education in new ways—ways that, we argue, can make college stronger and more accessible for all.

The potential of postsecondary education for creating change is apparent. Allen Thomas, in "I Did What They Said I Couldn't," writes about exceeding others' expectations of him. Before his college experience, he hadn't done things on his own and his socializing was limited, but he saw a lot of growth after attending higher education. Payton Storms, in "#CreatingMyOwnLife," reflects on her move from a rural town to a residential college experience at a large midwestern university. Along the way, she meets friends, navigates a complicated bus system, and demonstrates that she too belongs in college. Taylor Cathey, in "'BGWYN' and 'Confidence with Curves,'" also highlights a sense of belonging as she navigates an opportunity to explore her dreams with support and encouragement from many. These pieces demonstrate that, with often small but intentional supports, such as learning campus bus routes or how to connect to student groups, students with labels of intellectual disability are able to find their communities on campus and experience a sense of belonging. Inclusive programs can enable these connections not by creating separate opportunities for the students but by helping to advocate for students enrolled in their programs accessing the entire campus experience.

Creating Our Own Lives powerfully demonstrates that students with labels of intellectual disability are actively engaging and building community through participation in inclusive higher education programs. Students are not passively waiting for opportunities; rather, they are taking on barriers that prevent them from fully accessing all aspects of college. We know that our volume is only a small sampling of the multitudes of students in inclusive programs. We are excited to continue to learn from students in inclusive higher education programs as they narrate and express their truths and challenge us all to continue to work toward inclusive higher education *for all.*

Notes

1. Quoted in "What Does Independence Look Like?," Disability Network, July 1, 2022, https://www.dnswm.org/what-does-independence-look-like/.
2. Quoted in "Making a Better Space for Everyone," Sport Information Resource Centre, November 26, 2020, https://sirc.ca/news/making-a-better-space-for-everyone/.

Acknowledgments

This work has many pieces that took a long time to come to fruition. We are so grateful to our many authors, most of whom were college students when this process began and now are graduates or finishing their university programs. They are all brilliant writers, poets, artists, and makers. We appreciate the patience, persistence, and grace that these authors shared with us during this long process that bridged a pandemic and worked through multiple iterations of this published work. Their stories make clear the value of a college experience and the wealth that inclusion brings to higher education.

We would also like to thank those who shepherded this work: our editor, Pieter Martin, editorial assistant Anne Carter, Manifold digital projects editor Terence Smyre, and the entire team at the University of Minnesota Press. Bringing a work like this to publication is no small feat, especially in the world of academic publishing. We recognize the effort that was made to see value in work not often noticed by mainstream academia. It is what makes this work important but risky, and we are grateful for the support that was required.

We appreciate and recognize our colleagues in inclusive higher education and inclusive education writ large: those who are doing this work under the radar for fear of being noticed and asked to leave; those who are working with no real recognition or funding; those who are the only inclusive educators in their university, state, region, or country. We know that this work is just the beginning and we have seen it grow in unimaginable ways. We are so excited for the future.

Contributors

Makayla Adkins was born in Rowan County, North Carolina. She is a 2021 graduate of the Scholars with Diverse Abilities Program at Appalachian State University.

Olivia Baist is an alumnus (2022) of the InclusiveU program at Syracuse University, obtaining her certificate of completion in studio arts. Olivia identifies as having an intellectual disability and being disabled. During her freshman year of college, Olivia was featured in the documentary film *And They Were Roommates: Navigating Inclusive Mentorship in Higher Education.*

Brandon Baldwin is in his senior year of the Beyond Academics program at UNC Greensboro. His dream is to be a writer and motivator for others with disabilities.

George Barham is a senior in the Excel Program at Georgia Tech. He is from Atlanta, Georgia. George is interested in animation and graphic design and plans on working as a cartoon creator after graduation.

Marquavious Barnes is a senior in the Excel Program at Georgia Tech. He is from Athens, Georgia, and people call him Qua. His interest is in sports/customer service, and he plans to work at the University of Georgia or downtown Athens after graduation.

Katie Bartlett is a student at Washington State University. She likes taking classes in marching band, history, and math. Her favorite club on campus is country swing dancing and her favorite internship was at the WSU Veterinary Teaching Hospital.

Steven Brief has autism and creates videos and gives speeches on autism. His dream is to help change the world for the better and help individuals with autism and their parents. He has pages on YouTube and Facebook called Autism Explained by SB.

De'Onte Brown graduated from the IDEAL program at Georgia State University and obtained a certificate in film and digital media. He enjoys filming, creating, and editing videos.

Meghan Brozaitis graduated from InclusiveU at Syracuse University. She was a peer trainer and went with other InclusiveU students to basketball games and other campus events. She enjoys working with kids, going for walks, and taking pictures of sunsets and nature.

Mary Bryant is proud to be a mom to Kailin and Eilish Kelderman. She founded and is the director of the Path to Independence program for the Nevada Center for Excellence in Disabilities at the University of Nevada, Reno.

Gracie Carroll is a 2022 graduate of the Scholars with Diverse Abilities Program at Appalachian State University. Her story was written during her first semester. Since graduation, Gracie has worked full-time at Walmart and has been preparing to move from her home near the coast to Charlotte, North Carolina, where she will be able to spend more time with her sisters.

Taylor Cathey is a twenty-six-year-old, two-time graduate from the Roberts Wesleyan University BELL Program and the SUNY Geneseo LIVES Program. Taylor has autism. She lives with her mother in Leroy, New York, and plans to move out on her own. She is a freelance writer and enjoys all things involving creativity, feminism, and self-expression.

Maia Chamberlain is a junior at Syracuse University in the InclusiveU program. She lives with her family and commutes to school. Maia has cerebral palsy and is nonverbal. Usually she travels with her aide/interpreter and uses both sign language and Snap Core First on her iPad to communicate.

Antonio E. Contreras is a senior in the Georgia Tech Excel Program and has received the Laura Lee Leadership Award from the State of the Art Conference and is a former California ABLE ambassador. Antonio is originally from San Francisco, California, and moved 2,200 miles away from his family to attend college and live independently and inclusively with roommates. He loves playing intramural basketball, attending sports events all over campus and metro Atlanta with his friends, and working out. He recently adopted a cat named Ella.

Kim Dean is associate professor in the School of Education at Arcadia University and the REAL program faculty mentor. Her teaching and research focus on inclusion and building capacity in both K–12 and higher education communities for meaningful mental health literacy and inclusion for people with disabilities.

Elizabeth Droessler lives with her mom at their petting zoo in Wake Forest, North Carolina. She was adopted at age seven from Russia and has three brothers, one of whom was also adopted from the same orphanage in Russia. She graduated from Appalachian State University's Scholars with Diverse Abilities Program in 2020, where she was on the color guard team and took photos for the college newspaper. She works at her family's petting zoo and part time at Gabi's Grounds. She loves animals and working with children and older people.

Katie Ducett is a doctoral candidate in inclusive (special) education at Syracuse University. She holds bachelor's and master's degrees in chemistry education, special education, and literacy education from Nazareth College. She has numerous roles within the Taishoff Center for Inclusive Higher Education, including being on the executive planning committee for the annual national State of the Art Conference on inclusive higher education and the Student Leadership Conference.

Keiron Dyck has completed the Scholars with Diverse Abilities Program at Appalachian State University and the North Carolina Leadership Education in Neurodevelopmental Disorders program as a self-advocate. He hopes to have more chances to advocate for individuals with disabilities in the future.

Michael Gill is associate professor of disability studies at Syracuse University. He loves to ferment, get tattoos, eat spicy food, and cuddle with his dog.

Rachel Gomez is a senior in the Excel Program at Georgia Tech. They are from Short Hills, New Jersey. Rachel is interested in working in the medical field and plans on working as an x-ray technician assistant or an electrocardiograph technician assistant after graduation.

Deriq Graves is a graduate of the IDEAL program at Georgia State. Deriq is an exceptional storyteller, an animated character actor, and a skilled technical writer. Deriq spent his time at GSU studying film, scriptwriting, and acting and volunteering with the Alliance Theatre, Panther's Pantry, and the EXLAB.

Micah Gray graduated from Appalachian State University's Scholars with Diverse Abilities Program, where he majored in music. He has a passion for singing and traveling. Since his graduation, he has joined a gospel recording choir and traveled throughout the United States singing and praising God. He also works, but nothing gives him greater joy than singing with his choir.

Maggie Guillaume is a senior in the Excel Program at Georgia Tech. They are from Roswell, Georgia. Maggie is interested in volunteering and plans on working as a teacher assistant at an elementary school after graduation.

Cleo Hamilton is nice and friendly. He graduated on Mother's Day 2020 from Syracuse University. He was a 2019–20 Remembrance Scholar. He is a photographer and runs the Instagram page @cleohamiltonphotography. His favorite city is Brooklyn.

Nathan Heald is a lecturer and career development coordinator with the Excel Program at Georgia Tech. He teaches multiple courses related to career development and transition. He is interested in supporting students to realize their potential and find careers that fit their unique gifts.

Joshua R. Hourigan is a former Transition and Access Program student at the University of Cincinnati. He is continuing his education at Ivy Tech Community College's hospitality program as a pastry student hoping to start a business after he completes his studies. He enjoys spending time with family and friends, traveling, baking, playing and studying percussion, and making artwork.

Hannah Lenae Humes is a student in the Next Steps program at Vanderbilt University. She enjoys public speaking, traveling, going to music concerts, and being an advocate for inclusive education. Hannah wants to work in the music industry, as well as with young children. Hannah was born with Down syndrome or trisomy 21.

Courtney Jorgensen is part of the Aggies Elevated program at Utah State University. She works as an assistant teacher for children's theater classes and as a nanny. She volunteers as a self-advocate with the Utah Regional Leadership Education in Neurodevelopmental Disabilities organization. Her goals are to finish her Aggies Elevated program and to become a florist or a professional who works with children. Courtney would also like to get married and have her own family.

Eilish Kelderman is the proud younger sister of Kailin (KK). She recently completed her master's in social work degree and is a licensed social worker. She works as a program coordinator at the Nevada Center for Excellence in Disabilities Family Navigation Network at the University of Nevada, Reno.

Kailin Kelderman is a twenty-seven-year-old woman with Down syndrome. She is a graduate of the Path to Independence program at the University of Nevada, Reno. She continues to live on her own as she explores the world and finds herself.

Kenneth Kelty is an award-winning motivational speaker and writer on his life with disabilities and self-determination. He is an alumnus of Western Carolina University's two-year inclusive University Participant Program. He has spoken across the country, sharing his story at many universities and conferences. He is an active member of Tarheel Toastmasters, and he hopes to become an accredited speaker.

Kaelan Knowles was a part of the inclusive learning academy at Kennesaw State University. He graduated in 2020 and really enjoyed his time there. His favorite class during his time at Kennesaw was Japanese 1001. He enjoys learning different languages, such as Korean and ASL.

Karlee Lambert attends Appalachian State University, majoring in elementary education with a concentration in exceptional learners. She has a passion for education and young learners. She is excited to read this book and to see how inclusive higher education looks around the United States.

Kate Lisotta is a senior psychology major at Arcadia University who lives in New York and serves as a peer mentor for the REAL Certificate.

Rachel Mast is enrolled in the Missouri State University Bear POWER program and is a senator in the Student Government Association. She is a member of the National Down Syndrome Advocacy Coalition, an ABLE National Resource Center adviser, and has won the Laura Lee Self-Advocate Leadership Award. When not in college, she works as a hostess at the Olive Garden. Rachel is studying hospitality and acting and hopes to someday live in a pink house.

Elise McDaniel is on the path to achieving her dreams through the University of Tennessee FUTURE program. Known for being a hard worker, she has taken college by storm, evidenced by her selection as a student presenter at the 2019 State of the Art Conference on Inclusive Postsecondary Education and Individuals with Intellectual Disability. She is a world traveler, having been to China, Israel, Europe, Mexico, Hawaii, and the Caribbean. She loves Broadway, hip-hop dance, and music in general and loves to showcase her dance and karaoke skills. Elise aspires to have a career and live independently and is honored to show what someone with Down syndrome can do.

Emma Miller is a graduate of Appalachian State University. She is legally blind and attended the Scholars with Diverse Abilities Program to learn lots of new skills and do things independently. She loves to work with older adults in an assisted living facility by doing activities and entertainment. She loves to play the piano and sing. She loves going to Young Life and learning more about the Bible and having fun with her friends.

Jake Miller is a young man with autism. He lives at home with his mom and works several jobs in his community of Pittsford, New York. He is very social and loves spending time with his friends.

Beth Myers is a faculty member at Syracuse University and executive director of the Taishoff Center for Inclusive Higher Education. She loves working with InclusiveU, swimming, traveling, and crossword puzzles.

Lydia Newnum graduated from Appalachian State University with a bachelor of science in elementary education. She completed a second academic concentration in exceptional learners and acknowledges just how much she learned from volunteering as a peer support with the students who were part of the Scholars with Diverse Abilities Program. Lydia is currently completing a master's degree in reading education.

Brenna Mantz Nielsen has Asperger's syndrome. She has learned social skills to help her communicate with others. Brenna is a very determined person and compassionate. She just got married, and she graduated in the second cohort of the Aggies Elevated program. She works at the Institute for Disability Research, Policy, and Practice. Brenna has learned so much in her life and continues to strive toward catching her dreams.

Carly O'Connell is a student at Syracuse University's InclusiveU program. She enjoys learning about advocacy for people with disabilities like hers so that she can help people better understand others like herself in a more compassionate way.

Nadia Osbey graduated from the IDEAL program at Georgia State. Nadia is determined, independent, and kind. She works hard, plays hard, takes care of her friends, and enjoys artistic expression of all kinds. Majoring in music production, during her time at GSU Nadia created soundtracks, wrote her own songs, and learned what it takes to represent artists in the industry. Nadia is published in the *Signal,* GSU's student-run newspaper, and worked with Georgia State Athletics to gain sponsorships, promote ticket sales, plan events, and raise funds. Currently, she works security for the Mercedes-Benz Stadium.

Stirling Peebles works at Green Mountain Self-Advocates, a Vermont statewide nonprofit disability rights organization, and at the University of Vermont's Center on Disability and Community Inclusion as the dissemination assistant for the Think College Vermont program. Stirling is an alumnus of Think College Vermont and completed an eighteen-credit certificate with a concentration in film and media communications. She holds a human resources management certificate from Champlain College. Stirling was a self-advocate Leadership Education in Neurodevelopmental Disabilities (LEND) fellow and a teaching assistant in Vermont LEND.

Breyan Pettaway is a graduate from the IDEAL program at Georgia State. He is a talented artist and writer. He has a wide creative scope and scale to his works, coupled with a meticulous writing process. Breyan has a wealth of random facts and knowledge that he is ready to break any silence with. Breyan has a published article in the GSU student-run newspaper, the *Signal*. He has a variety of experiences in job positions and locations, such as food service, airport staff, and column writing.

Amanda Pilkenton is a senior in the Excel Program at Georgia Tech. She is from Brookhaven, Georgia. Amanda is interested in biology, psychology, and space sciences. She loves drawing and hanging out with her family and friends. Amanda plans on working as an elementary school teacher's assistant after graduation.

True Rafferty is a senior in the Excel Program at Georgia Tech. He is from Atlanta, Georgia. True is interested in warehousing operations and plans on working as a forklift operator after graduation.

Taylor Ruppe is a graduate of the Scholars with Diverse Abilities Program at Appalachian State University. Taylor worked at the student union during her time at AppState and volunteered at an afterschool program.

Lawrence Sapp has completed his sophomore year at the University of Cincinnati in Ohio and hopes to work in the field of architectural engineering upon graduation. He is a competitive swimmer and a member of the Team USA Paralympic Swimming team. Notable achievements are a gold medal in the one-hundred-meter backstroke at the World Para Swimming Championships in Mexico City in 2017 and a silver medal in the one-hundred-meter butterfly at the World Para Swimming Championships in London in 2019. He lives with his family and loves to travel, play video games, construct buildings with Legos, and hang out with friends.

Tyler Shore is a graduate of the Scholars with Diverse Abilities Program at Appalachian State University. He loves music, theater, schedules, and mindfulness breathing practices. Tyler works as a DJ at the campus radio station and at Belk Library and Information Commons.

Brianna Silva graduated from the Scholars with Diverse Abilities Program. Her story was written during her first semester of college.

Alex Smith is a senior in the Excel Program at Georgia Tech. They are interested in maps and travel and plan on working at a front desk at a hotel or as a GIS technician after graduation.

Elliott Smith is a senior in the Excel Program at Georgia Tech. They are interested in becoming an educator and plan on working as a teacher's assistant after graduation.

Phillandra Smith is assistant professor of special education and critical disability studies at the University of Pittsburgh. Her research interests include the intersections of race and disability in teacher preparation and inclusive higher education. She loves collecting and caring for plants.

Payton Storms is a student at the University of Kansas and has lived in Lawrence for two years. She hopes that everyone loves her story and finds it inspirational and interesting to read and that it is very relatable to many people.

Allen Thomas attended Appalachian State University's Scholars with Diverse Abilities Program. He is in his last year at Wake Tech and wants to transfer back to Appalachian State to finish his degree in special education.

Kylie Walter earned her BS in inclusive elementary and special education from Syracuse University while also minoring in disability studies. Kylie was a residential mentor for Syracuse University's InclusiveU program. For her undergraduate honors thesis, she filmed and produced a participatory and reflexive documentary, titled *And They Were Roommates: Navigating Inclusive Mentorship in Higher Education.* The award-winning film provides insight into inclusive mentorship and has been shared at conferences and film festivals around the world.

Stephen Wanser is a second-year REAL Certificate student at Arcadia University who loves creative writing.

Sayid Webb is a graphic designer, cosplayer, student assistant, gamer, and creative student. He hosted a Halloween and a Christmas party at the IDEAL program. Sayid creates flyers and posters for events and meetings and is a talented student with a creative mind who gets things done.

Breana Whittlesey graduated from Kennesaw State University with a major in early childhood education. She has ADHD. She loves working with kids and hopes to become a student teacher.

Luke Wilcox graduated from the Scholars with Diverse Abilities Program at Appalachian State University. Luke is a young man with cerebral palsy who uses an electric wheelchair for mobility and a Tobii Dynavox speech-generating device to speak in a cowboy accent. Luke is an aspiring author and true friend to many.

Adam Wolfond is a nonspeaking autistic artist, poet, and presenter. He is the cofounder of the A Collective (renamed Disassembly) in Toronto, where he also works in visual art and poetry. His film and artwork can be viewed at https://www.esteerelation.com. Adam is interested in the movement of language (which he refers to as "languaging") and expression and how neurotypical language forms delimit neurodiverse expression. His poetry has been featured on https://poets.org. His chapbook of poetry, *In Way of Music Water Answers Toward Questions Other Than What Is Autism,* is available through his publisher, Unrestricted Interest.

Made in United States
Orlando, FL
27 December 2023

41686662R00153